# Entering The Heart

## Flann Lynch OFM Cap

First published in 2011 by Messenger Publications

2nd Edition, 2013.

Messenger Publications
37 Lower Leeson Street, Dublin 2
www.messenger.ie

Printed in Ireland

ISBN 978-1-872245-81-2

Cover designed by Messenger Publications Design Department
Inside designed by Kieran Shorten
Typeset in 10/12.5 Times New Roman and Apple Chancery

MESSENGER
PUBLICATIONS
JESUITS in IRELAND

# Table of Contents

# Introduction

L ife for many is a difficult or impossible riddle, a tangled web of unanswered questions. Inevitably people will ask questions, many, many questions. Answers need to be attempted. Maps are needed to give us an understanding of who we are, why we are here, and what the way forward consists of. Tools are needed to empower us if we are to embark on the journey, be equipped to deal with the difficulties, and continue to make progress.

Why can't life be free of struggle and breakdown, terror and tragedy, free of pain and disease, suffering and death? Why can't the world be free of crisis after crisis, free of greed, injustice and oppression, free of the violence and destruction of war?

Why can't our homes be stress-free and all our relationships be harmonious? Why can't we live to be old without the services of medical experts? Why can't we depart this earth in peace, free of all fear and guilt? Who is in charge? Who has plunged us into this impossible chaos?

A God of love could not be responsible. Equally, a God of love will take responsibility for healing, transforming and unifying the human race. A God of love would never want us to suffer, would have the deepest respect and esteem for each and every person, and would create the person in freedom.

Freedom is a most astonishing gift, but it has deep and far-reaching consequences when misused. Unfortunately for us all, the first people God created, Adam and Eve, misused their freedom, knowingly doing wrong, setting off a chain reaction that would affect all people of all time. Science shows how we are all prisoners of the genetic pool we have inherited.

Adam and Eve's sin filled them with fear and guilt which are the source of mental, emotional and physical illness, as well as all the other evils that plague the human race. Their sin also created the false self, the split between the false self and the true self, the split between mind and body, and the dualism that separates us from self, God, others and creation.

Our task consists of healing the split, healing and integrating the person, and unifying the human race. Humanly, the task is impossible, and if we feel we have only a minimum of faith, it will be enough to give us a starting point. We can launch out and go forward in hope, allowing ourselves to be surprised by how exhilarating the adventure can be.

i

# An Overview

This book is about attitudes, the great signposts of life. It focuses mainly on the eight Beatitudes, blessed are the gentle, the just, the peacemakers, etc. Readers are given an understanding and an experience of each Beatitude, and shown how to apply them in everyday life. The book has grown out of the Vision seminar, attended by over twenty thousand people over the last sixteen years.

When St. Francis responded to the invitation of Christ to 'repair my Church', a new revolution transformed the Church from the ground upwards. We need a similar revolution today, giving people a powerful experience of Christ, and his teaching on the Beatitudes.

Why are the Beatitudes so important? A Jesuit missionary, observing that Catholics killed Catholics in Rwanda, asked 'did our Catholic education ever make sense? He suggested that the life of the Beatitudes is the missing link in our faith formation. The Beatitudes are central because they form our conscience with a strong sense of compassion and gentleness, justice and peace. The Beatitudes are loving attitudes, the be-attitudes that enable us to be who we are, the true self God created us to be,

It is widely accepted today that people have a strong spiritual hunger. The spirituality of the Beatitudes is a very powerful way of feeding that hunger. Good spirituality seeks to find God in everyday experience, and has three elements: knowledge, experience and expression. We need the knowledge and understanding that will enable us to develop and deepen an authentic relationship with God. Knowledge of the Beatitudes leads us to the God of love, and to the mind or thinking of Christ.

Experience, the second element of spirituality, consists of bringing the head knowledge into the heart, where it becomes a lived experience. When knowledge is confined to the intellect, it never touches our lives in a way that arouses passion and inspires action. That is why it is crucial that our knowledge and understanding of God become integrated into our emotional life. Expression, the third element of spirituality, flows automatically from experience into inspiring and powerful action.

The book attempts to give readers an understanding of the Beatitudes, an experience of their power, and the commitment to be in action, bringing compassion, peace and justice to the world. Opening up a vision of unlimited possibility, readers are given the tools to transform both themselves and the world.

The last page gives guidelines for small group meetings, and guidelines also for groups to study the book in a way that is experiential rather than academic, sharing experience rather than discussing.

# The Eight Beatitudes

*How blessed are the poor in spirit:*

*theirs is the kingdom of heaven.*

*Blessed are those who mourn:*

*they shall be comforted.*

*Blessed are the gentle:*

*they shall have the earth for their heritage.*

*Blessed are those who hunger and thirst for what is right:*

*they shall be satisfied.*

*Blessed are the merciful: they shall have mercy shown them.*

*Blessed are the pure in heart:*

*they shall see God.*

*Blessed are the peacemakers:*

*they shall be called sons and daughters of God.*

*Blessed are those who are persecuted in the cause of right:*

*theirs is the kingdom of heaven.*

# Life is Attitude

L ife is attitude. We are our attitudes. Success and contentment depend on attitude. We see ourselves, others, life and God through the lens of our attitudes. We relate to life largely through the particular attitudes with which we have grown up.

Attitudes are an ever-present mindset, determining how we think, feel, listen, speak and behave. They are either loving or negative, life-enhancing or damaging, inspiring or undermining. They consist of beliefs, conversation and feelings, that become attitudes when they are deeply ingrained or habitual.

Attitudes flowing from beliefs include loving attitudes such as, 'I'm precious to God', and 'life is opportunity', as opposed to 'I'm not good enough', and 'life is hard'. In conversation we have the loving attitudes of praising and encouraging, and the negative attitudes of blaming and complaining, etc. And we can have feelings that are attitudes of either generosity and compassion, or aggression and selfishness, etc.

Attitudes act as filters for both our love and generosity and our prejudices and ignorance. An attitude needs to be changed when it is not respectful of self, others life or God, or when it is not loving or life-giving. 'The remarkable thing is that we have a choice every day regarding the attitude we will embrace for that day ... we are in charge of our attitudes.'

Recognising our need to change, Christ invited us to repent, to re-pent or re-think, be willing to change our minds, our attitudes, when they are unreasonable or disempowering. He then gave us a set of loving attitudes or values that we call the eight Beatitudes *(Matthew 5: 1-12)*. To those who would embrace these loving attitudes, he promised a blessed state of mind and heart. This would include great gifts in plenty, especially the most precious of all, deep inner peace. 'My peace I leave you, my own peace I give you, a peace the world cannot give, that is my gift to you' *(John 14:27)*.

Since attitudes are the very bedrock of life, everything depends on their quality: our emotional stability, confidence, self-esteem, the wellness of mind, feelings, body and spirit, the success of our relationships, work, career, the use of our gifts, caring for others, a sense of justice, etc.

What is necessary is that we be willing to stop and look at how selfish or self-defeating some of our attitudes can be. This is a great place at which to arrive. Now we are humble enough to admit to our helplessness, and open enough to allow God to help us embark on a new adventure, the way of love. What is on offer is an exciting and empowering way of living, a vision of life that is truly inspiring.

***Invitation:*** *I can change my attitudes. What freedom!*

1

# The Promise

People are spiritual beings having a human experience, a bodily, earthly experience. We arrived just a few moments ago and we stay for a few more before departing to our permanent existence, leaving our bodies behind. If our stay is so short and eternity is forever, is it not urgent that we have a balanced perspective on life, giving priority to the spiritual?

St. Paul points to the three things that last: 'faith, hope and love, and the greatest of these is love.' Love is central because it is the great reality that gives our earthly existence meaning, harmony and enjoyment, and makes our departure peaceful and hope-filled. The task is to understand the meaning of love, making it the heart and centre of life.

We are greatly empowered by the promise of Christ to be with us always - with us now in this present moment, always, moment by moment until our last breath. He has told us that the purpose of his presence is to love and support us with an abundance of what we need. He invites us to a relationship of deep intimacy and friendship. It is through this relationship that we experience his love and support, and that we are empowered to live the love outlined in the Beatitudes.

The blessed state of mind and heart, promised by this way of love, is so attractive and compelling, that we need to explore and uncover the hidden power of each Beatitude. As we engage in this task, we experience the three Fs of love: freedom, fruitfulness and fulfilment. Freedom from everything that limits us, and freedom to make a difference in the lives of others, which is *fruitfulness,* the second F of love.

The experience of giving love wholeheartedly gives our lives great meaning, making us deeply fulfilled, which is the third F of love. And so we discover through practice and experience that Christ can be trusted absolutely in the promises he makes.

The particular approach we use here helps us to move from a place of knowing in our minds to a place of inner knowing in our hearts. At this level an inspiring vision of God, and of what love can do, opens up. We move from seeing life as difficult or as a problem, to seeing it as a great and wonderful mystery that is always unfolding.

Horizons widen and attitudes are transformed as awareness and possibilities constantly expand. We learn to live more and more in the now of the present moment, responding with love to the opportunity that each moment presents. We discover that this is the prized place to be. And we see change as essential and desirable in our growth towards enlightenment for which the heart hungers.

***Invitation:*** *Today I'm inspired by what is possible.*

*Inspired by Love*

*making us*

*free*

*fruitful*

*fulfilled*

# A Vision to Inspire

Our greatest fear is that when we die life will come to a sudden and abrupt end. Our greatest hope, on the other hand, is that when we cross the threshold of death, a glorious and perfect world will fill our horizons. We have a deep hunger to be welcomed and embraced by the God of love, and to reunite with family members, friends and all others in relationships of the deepest love and friendship.

The New Testament reveals a radical and stunning picture of the hereafter. At the centre of this vision stands the God whose love is infinite and unconditional. The vision of heaven spelled out by St. Paul brings delight to our hearts. We see it overflowing with such bliss and ecstasy that ' Eye has not seen, nor ear heard, nor has it ever entered the human heart the good things God has prepared for those that love him' *(1 Corinthians 2:9)*. Paul's glimpse of heaven is also that of many others who were given this gift.

The critical question asks how are we to grow into a deeper awareness and experience of this vision? The practice of love needs to be central to the project because God is love, and we, in our essence, are also love. So it is our nature, our deepest desire, to give and receive love. The eight Beatitudes provide us with a comprehensive understanding of love, and its transformative power.

Our ability to love receives its power from our relationship with Jesus because this relationship connects us with the source of all love. We can encounter Jesus continually in what we can call his four great qualities or faces: goodness, beauty, unity and truth. These aspects mirror his presence and his all-encompassing love.

We see goodness everywhere, especially in the generosity of people and in mother earth. Beauty, always new, always unique, fills the universe. When we are aware we feel the nearness of Jesus, and a sense of belonging, in a love-filled, peak-experience world. Loving awareness feeds and expands our vision, as does the miraculous order and unity of the universe.

Jesus is like the master conductor of the orchestra, bringing clock-work precision to the earth orbiting the sun, to night following day and to the seasons. Our experience of goodness, beauty and unity, demonstrates the truth of Jesus who cares so deeply: 'I go to prepare a place for you so that where I am (heaven), you may be too' *(John 14:3)*.

The pursuit of the Christian vision brings about a deep-seated change of attitude, filling us with wonder and gratitude, and an experience of the joys of love: freedom, fruitfulness and fulfilment. Our deepest hunger is satisfied, and we find inspiring answers to life's great questions.

***Invitation:*** *The future offers us more than we could ever imagine.*

4

# The Adventure

The human situation is such that we are pulled in opposite directions by opposing forces. On the one hand, the influences of love are drawing us into a world of infinite abundance. This is a world of constantly expanding possibility, a world of goodness, beauty, unity and truth. It is God's world, and it is also the world of the true self. On the other hand, we have the forces that create and feed the false self, fear, worry, complaining, etc. These energies are pulling us into a world of suffering, making our lives miserable.

Fear of the unknown keeps us trapped inside the boxed-in world of the false self. We have many other fears, including the fear of losing control, and of losing our hard-earned security. A measure of security is necessary. It is the fear and attachment that create the problem. How much better to find lasting security in deep surrender to the God of love. Surrender becomes easier as we keep discovering how unconditional God's love is for us all. The continuing discovery, deepening our faith, is the key to keeping us on track in our journey of faith.

The Scriptures are a wonderful means of constantly discovering God anew. In the book of Deutoronomy we read of the tenderness of God's loving care: 'He found him in the wilderness, in fearful, desolate wastes. He surrounded him, he lifted him up, he kept him as the apple of his eye. Like an eagle that watches over its nest, that hovers over its young, so he spread his wings, he took him, placed him on his outstretched wings' *(Deuternomy 32:11-12)*.

God found the Jewish people in the wilderness, in the slavery of Egypt, and in their own slavery to sin. Similarly, he finds us in our wilderness, the negative world of the false self, with its slavish attachment to negative, sinful ways. Like the Jewish people, God cherishes us as the apple of his eye, protecting and caring for us like the eagle that hovers over its young. The mother eagle feeds its young until it knows it is time for it to leave its nest. Then with a fish in her mouth she circles the nest, tempting its offspring to overstretch, lose its balance and fall out of the nest. Eventually she succeeds. The young eagle, terrified, falls like a stone through the air. After several seconds it moves its wings, and discovers it can fly. In an instant it goes from terror to delight, from despair to ecstasy.

What will move us out of our 'nest', wean us off our attachment to earthly securities, change our fearful, selfish attitudes? Continuing to discover God's love at a deeper level, noticing its presence everywhere, brings about a great growth in trust and surrender. Each of the eight Beatitudes gives us a deep experience of the three Fs of love, freedom, fruitfulness and fulfilment. Because love is everything, the only reality, we need to make it the great priority in our life's adventure.

***Invitation:*** *Thank you, Jesus, for the comfort of your presence.*

# Creating the Future

As Jesus wants us to enjoy the bliss of heaven, so he also wants us to be happy and fulfilled on this earth. If our lives are to have meaning and fulfilment, then we need to embrace the two great life-giving realities. The first is that Jesus, in his love and generosity, is our constant friend and companion. The second is that he empowers us to live a life of love with its rewards of freedom, fruitfulness and fulfilment.

Nothing serves us better than to strengthen our faith as we keep discovering what St. Paul calls 'The breadth and length, and height and depth' *(Eph.3:14)* of God's love. A growing faith is the foundation and source of all meaning and fulfilment.

We will be richly rewarded by giving special attention to the following distinctions because they do so much to develop our faith: the perspective that sees love as infinitely abundant; feeling supported by the countless people who live lives of extraordinary compassion and generosity; learning to grow into an ever-deepening attitude of trust and surrender.

The gift of perspective, giving us a balanced view, is one of life's great essentials, keeping us on course in our daily adventure. We could easily allow ourselves to get embittered by the pain of life, or we could react with cynicism to the world's ills: poverty, injustice, violence, corruption, selfishness, etc. Perspective shows us that no matter how great the world's pain and evil, it is still limited, whereas the love and goodness of God are infinitely abundant. 'Where sin abounded, grace abounded all the more.'

The words 'all the more' express the expanding nature of God's goodness. Jesus is always at hand with overflowing generosity, especially when we need him most. If we ponder this perspective in the heart, then we feel free of the burden of what might happen, and inspired by a future alive with possibility. Doors will open and opportunities will present themselves. Our perspective is greatly strengthened by the awareness that countless people, individuals, families and groups, are outstanding models of love and commitment. The awareness of such widespread support strengthens the perspective that love will always prevail over the forces of pain and evil.

Why don't we trust? Hasn't Providence always taken care of us? If so, why worry about the future? Jesus invites us to learn from nature, the birds, the flowers, etc. We are always at the fork of the road, with one sign pointing to the road of fear and worry, the other, to the road of trust. Worry destroys us, trust gives us everything, and abundantly. Life is a decision. We can choose to trust as easily as we choose to worry. We then grow into an attitude of deep trust, and surrender to Providence, causing our new perspective to be wonderfully enhanced. (This theme is developed in the sixth Beatitude).

*Invitation: I find great freedom in the new perspective.*

6

# Light and Darkness

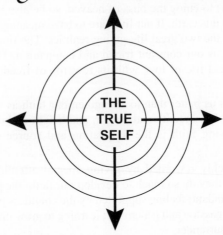

THE
TRUE
SELF

The above diagram illustrates how the true self in each of us is surrounded by layers or circles of darkness that occupy our awareness for much of our waking hours. These layers of darkness are what Carl Jung called the shadow side of ourselves. They consist of the energy, used negatively, that feeds the false self. We can distinguish many kinds of darkness.

We have the darkness of 'I'm not good enough', 'I'm not lovable', the darkness of scarcity: no love, no support, no confidence, no time no opportunity, no money, the darkness of 'it's hard', and 'I can't'. We also include the darkness of regretting, of blaming and complaining, of criticising and judging. And there is the darkness of fear, worry and anxiety, of anger and impatience, of bitterness and resentment, the darkness of greed, envy and jealousy, of lust, use, abuse and betrayal, of violence and suffering, of injustice and oppression, etc. Hell, in its varying degrees, consists of giving our awareness to any of the above.

The arrows in the diagram show the movement or flow of love from the true self to others. The movement of this love is generated by powerful spiritual tools, such as wonder and gratitude, the listening ear and the kind word, the Gentle Lifestyle, trust and surrender, the humble prayer, etc. As the love flows it dissolves the layers of darkness, restoring to the true self the energy used up in these layers. The flow of love is what forgives, heals and reconciles. It makes us compassionate, gentle and humble. It fills us with a passion for justice and peace. Love is the transforming energy that integrates, making us whole and complete. Love is the power of God that unifies the human race.

*Invitation: Lord, fill us with the light of your wisdom and love.*

7

# Childhood Trauma

Some find it hard to get started on their spiritual journey, others feel they are making little progress. A childhood trauma, never dealt with, could be the cause. A trauma disempowers because it damages our confidence and self-esteem. A child, asked to read at the age of six, was deeply humiliated when the class laughed at her. She was unable to stand up for herself as an adult, and suffered dreadfully at the hands of an abusive husband. Having discovered God's love, she found the strength to change her situation.

An intelligent boy, having failed an examination, felt deeply ashamed. He spent his life trying to prove himself until he was helped in middle age by a therapist. A girl was overlooked for the lead role in a school musical. Deeply hurt, she concluded that life should always be a struggle

A boy was unjustly accused of injuring his uncle, leaving him with low self-esteem and a fear of people. These examples show how a childhood trauma can leave people trapped in a world of pain and fear. Without a solution, it is impossible for life to be the dance or celebration Jesus means it to be. Many people can be affected. That is why it could be very helpful to identify a time in our childhood when we felt humiliated.

We ask simply: can I remember the most hurtful experience I had as a child? We then ask: what did the experience do to me? Or: what meaning did I give the experience? When we identify the painful event we see what the child saw. We see that it was a decision made only by the child, with a child's understanding. The moment we make this discovery we experience a new freedom. We can now stand in a new place, making adult choices, and allowing God to give us what we need. With great gentleness we forgive our inner child, and everyone else involved in the incident. If we have difficulty in forgiving, we may find help in the pages on the Beatitude of mercy.

Our need is to be healed, to grow in confidence and self-esteem, and in appreciation of our God-given worth. Our journey can be a slow and difficult one, yet very necessary and worthwhile. We need to be patient and gentle with ourselves as we work through our pain in our journey towards healing and wholeness. Discovering, in later pages, the tender mercy of Jesus and our God-given magnificence, will greatly enhance our self-esteem.

It is helpful to keep in mind that opportunity is the gift hidden in everything painful or difficult. We can find great comfort and strength in feeling the wonder of our being, and in opening our hearts in prayer, surrendering to the gentle Christ within. Times of silence are also a very necessary gift we need to give ourselves. This reflective approach to life helps us to grow into more loving attitudes towards self, others, life and Christ.

***Invitation:*** *Life is opportunity.*

# Mystery Unfolding

Mystery is a world beyond what we know, see or understand. We say that God is mystery because God is infinite and therefore unknowable. Mystery is like an infinite roll of map: the more we unroll it, the more we discover. The sense of mystery makes life an adventure, with discovery a constant occurrence. Without a sense of mystery, life becomes static, and everyone and everything always stay the same. Boredom sets in and meaning deserts us.

A sense of mystery evokes wonder, and a hunger to explore. Wonder is what enables us to penetrate the mystery, causing it to unfold, yielding up some of its secrets. When we have an eye for mystery, creation will unfold the mystery of God's glory: 'The heavens proclaim the glory of God, and the firmament shows forth the work of his hands' *(Psalm 19:1)*.

Mystery is an awesome reality beneath the surface: in people, in the events and circumstances of life, and in creation. Mystery invites us to be aware and to wonder, to listen and to ponder, to wait and to surrender. 'Be still and know that I am God,' which is to say, that as we let go and surrender, the mystery of God will unfold. We will experience the living Jesus and the current of his love, present beneath appearances.

The poet Rilke points to the necessity of patience in our journey into mystery. 'Be patient towards all that is unsolved in your heart . . . try to love the questions themselves like locked rooms, and like books that are written in a very foreign tongue ... Live the question now,' Rilke advises. The challenge is to live the mystery of what is as yet unresolved, and to trust that 'all things come to those who wait,' especially the peace of acceptance. When we wait in patience we learn to trust, that in due course, we will arrive at Mother Julian's insight: 'all will be well, and all will be well, and all manner of thing will be well.'

We have a great need to cultivate a patient silence, having silent moments and longer silences. Silence reveals the sacred as the mystery unfolds. Silence enables us to continue to be with the mystery, so awesome, so wondrous, so life-giving. In the presence of mystery we listen, ponder and wonder with a humble, grateful heart. So far beyond our comprehension, we can only wonder, trust and wait. Open to whatever mystery reveals, we accept, let go and surrender. What there is to do is to listen and wonder, to ponder and wonder, to wait and wonder, to surrender and wonder. So we wonder and wonder as the mystery of Christ, of love, of self and others, of pain and suffering, and of life, unfold in their own way, and in their own time. In the presence of mystery, we journey more deeply into the joys of love: freedom, fruitfulness and fulfilment.

***Invitation:*** *The sense of mystery expands my world.*

# Responding to Opportunity

Opportunities are great gifts, the building blocks of life. Often challenging, they are as essential to our journey as the air we breathe. They enable us, when we use them, to respond in love to life as it unfolds, and to use and develop our gifts. Life's journey, however, is strewn with lost opportunities. Recognising and responding to opportunity is what makes success possible in every area of life.

We need an ever-watchful eye for opportunity if we are to make the most of life. We can learn from the humble snail. Happy with its slow progress, it teaches us to be content with life. We can be so obsessed with results that the destination may be the only thing that counts. But the snail tells us that it is the journey that gives us the opportunities, moment by moment.

Opportunity is the axis on which life turns. When we take advantage of the daily opportunities, we will achieve much freedom, fruitfulness and fulfilment. If, however, we allow the lost opportunities to accumulate, then our life will grind towards a standstill. It is easy, if we are aware, to see the opportunity, and respond in love and gratitude to the non-stop miracle of life.

The key question is always: what is the opportunity in this moment? When we find life an uphill struggle, however, we may not find it easy to see the opportunity. At such times it is critical that we recognise that opportunity is the hidden gift in every difficult or painful situation. The habit of asking the key question will usually come to our rescue, and the opportunity will become apparent to us.

If a situation is very traumatic or painful, we can usually avail of a number of opportunities. We can allow others to help and support us. We can be gentle with ourselves, careful not to be critical of self, others, God or what the future holds. Complaining or criticising gives us short-term comfort and pleasure. Then we become miserable again, even more miserable. It is only when we respond in love to the opportunity that we achieve inner peace. We also have the opportunity of opening our hearts to Jesus, allowing him to give us peace and strength. And we can start to ask the key question: what is the opportunity here?

The human problem is one of awareness. Life can so easily pass us by. That is why we need to keep awakening constantly to both the gift and the necessity of opportunity. Attitudes are always changing for the better as we respond in love to the opportunities that present themselves.

Each moment presents us with the opportunity to let our love flow as we listen, speak and act with an open, generous heart. Gentle, kind and helpful, we thank God for countless blessings, and we often ask the key question, what opportunity is the present moment offering me?

**Invitation:** *I find opportunity in the moment.*

# The Three-Fold Path

Enlightenment is the state of living in the light of the risen Christ, guided and inspired by the seven gifts of the Holy Spirit: wisdom, understanding, counsel, fortitude, knowledge, devotion and reverence for God and the sacred. According to the saints, enlightenment consists of three key practices; prayer, loving service and penance or discipline. These practices are daily essentials as we build attitudes of love and generosity.

Prayer opens the heart, creating sacred space for the Holy Spirit to heal us in our brokenness, to bring about union with Jesus, and to expand our hearts with love for the world. Authentic prayer will always make us more gentle, more humble, more caring, and more just, especially towards the poor, and those in greatest need. Prayer is an absolute essential if we are to grow daily into a deeper living of the love and commitment presented in the Beatitudes.

Like prayer, loving service also opens and expands the heart for the flow of God's love. By showing us how to love and inspiring us to be in action, the eight Beatitudes bring about deep transformation in ourselves and in others. This transformation is particularly noticeable in our relationships, and in the way we feel and care for others. The use of any of the other tools, outlined throughout this book, also deepen our love and generosity, and our desire, and willingness, to put ourselves at the service of others.

We embrace penance or discipline, the third key practice, as the grace, the gift, that controls or sometimes eliminates the selfish attitudes and preoccupations that are often habitual and sometimes addictive. Discipline is the staying power that keeps us focused and responsible in our daily commitments. Discipline resists the temptation to get lukewarm or give up. If discipline is weak, then our power to pray and to love is seriously undermined. Like a muscle, the more we use it, the stronger discipline becomes. Constant practice strengthens the will, enabling us to be in charge of our lives, controlling selfish desires, and building the strength to commit and to love. We need to see discipline as a most essential gift we give ourselves.

The three great powers, prayer, loving service and discipline, give us a balanced and successful life. They work together but not independently, with each supporting and generating the other two. They lead us into God's world of abundant love and peace, into a state of deeper awareness, of enlightenment. At one with God, humanity and creation, we experience the joys of freedom, fruitfulness and fulfilment. The adventure is life-long, and in spite of many mistakes, always successful and fulfilling, when we give ourselves to it wholeheartedly.

*Invitation: I love and appreciate my three-fold gift.*

# Emotional Intelligence

In the past we equated intelligence with IQ, the brain power that tops the class, achieving the highest qualifications and the best jobs. Another, and even more important, intelligence has now been identified, what is called emotional intelligence. It can be defined simply as the ability to respond appropriately to life as it occurs. The test comes when the circumstances are difficult or painful. Emotional intelligence includes a wide range of standards, values and skills, the practise of which, enables us to turn what is stressful into opportunity.

Unlike the IQ, fixed at about the age of four, we can keep on improving our emotional intelligence throughout our lives. The Beatitudes provide the perfect context, giving us the values and the tools to respond to the countless daily opportunities to grow and develop. The practice of the first Beatitude, detaching us from negative preoccupations, creates the openness to accept the unbounded love Christ has for us, and to enter into a growing relationship of love and trust with him. In touch with the source of love, we find that we bring a depth of acceptance and patience to our relationships and to our daily tasks.

Openness also enables us to establish another powerful cornerstone of emotional intelligence: respect for the person. Accepting who we are, priceless words of love spoken by God, we learn to see every person in this deeply respectful light, relating to them accordingly. The habit of listening with love gives us direct access to the heart, the place of intuition, of wisdom and understanding. Through this listening we connect and empathise easily with people. Loving words and kind acts follow automatically, and our emotional intelligence deepens wonderfully.

The use of the Abundance Prayer, generating the love of all the Beatitudes, deepens our experience of Christ and his love, enabling us to overcome the urge to react with anger or impatience, or with fear, worry or anxiety, when an upset occurs. Instead, we learn to respond with patience and resilience, with acceptance and tolerance, and with mercy and compassion. What we have here is emotional intelligence at its best, always appropriate, always reconciling, always the peacemaker, creating communities of love.

Living the Gentle Lifestyle is a powerful stimulator of all the ingredients that cause emotional intelligence to grow. They include love, wonder and gratitude, patience and tolerance, confidence and self-esteem, strength and surrender, etc. Stands, or commitments (Sixth Beatitude), move the world, and move us powerfully into God's world where everything is abundant, especially the three Fs of love, freedom, fruitfulness and fulfilment, causing emotional intelligence to flourish. We stand in wonder and gratitude at the miracle of this most precious gift.

***Invitation:*** *I use every opportunity to build emotional intelligence.*

# The Genius of the Heart

Scientists have recently discovered what poets and mystics have always known: the heart has intelligence just like the brain. 'The heart has its reasons which reason does not know,' wrote Pascal. We find the same understanding in Christian spirituality. The Jesus prayer, for example, dating from the fourth century, and used mostly in the Orthodox Churches, was also called the prayer of the heart.

The heart was seen both as the centre of love and the place where Jesus resides. And so in the practice of the prayer, people were taught to centre their awareness in the heart. The heart then is the place where relationship with Jesus takes place. It is where we experience his love and support, and where union or oneness with him takes place.

The heart is also the place from which love can flow powerfully to one's own life, to one's relationships and to the world at large. The mind, with its dualistic thinking, sees everyone and everything as separate from us: me and you, me and God, me and the world. Until we surrender and live from the heart, we cannot connect deeply, and achieve the experience of oneness with Jesus, self, others and creation. This oneness is the sense of belonging for which our hearts hunger.

Western people tend to live almost entirely from the head. Neglect of the heart results in deep and widespread dysfunction, most notably in relationships, and in mental, emotional and physical health. The heart keeps us grounded in reality, in the present moment, where we see clearly the need or opportunity, and respond to it in love.

The head, on the other hand, tends to take us into a world of unreality where we lose our perspective. This is the busy world of endless distractions, where we relive the pain and regrets of the past, and worry about what might happen in the future.

The discovery of the intelligent heart is one of the greatest breakthroughs of our time. It gives us the joy of knowing that we have a heart that has intelligence, that it is the centre of abundant love and emtional intelligence, and that within it we encounter the person of Jesus.

Seen in this new light, the heart is a most astonishing miracle and gift. It presents us with exciting possibilities for enriching our lives, our relationships and our prayer. A great miracle takes place when we listen with the heart, with love, to the love in the heart of another person. The moment we do this, the love in us flows to the heart of that person, activating their love, if they are well disposed, and causing it to flow to us. The result is a heart to heart relationship, which is a relationship of love. We can practice this with people who are present or absent.

We need to be aware of how much we can neglect the heart. When everyday problems or difficulties arise, we can often react, becoming fearful, worried or stressed. Or we can become angry, wanting to punish and inflict pain. Or we may feel unable to forgive a real or perceived injustice. Or it might just be a case of disliking a person for no apparent reason.

What makes these situations so difficult is that the mind or thinking of the false self takes over. The true self, however, is always asking: what does my heart think? When we ask that question and listen in silence for a while, the heart will give us wise, loving and peaceful solutions.

## SOURCE OF LOVE

'What does my heart think?' needs to become the most important question in our daily lives, especially when problems arise. The habit of asking this question trains us to listen to, and live from the heart. As we live from the heart, giving and receiving love, we experience the three Fs of love: freedom from self-induced and unnecessary suffering; fruitfulness, making a much bigger difference in the lives of others, as the love flows freely and constantly from our hearts; fulfilment, experiencing a deep sense of inner peace, of belonging and support, as we connect with Jesus and with people.

It is worth noting that Mother Teresa often told people that each of us has enough love for the whole world. Imagine one's heart having enough love for the seven billion people on the planet, one by one, by one. How amazing! This is the truth that will set us free, accepting with joy and gratitude that 'Of his fullness (of God's love) we have all received.'

The heart has unlimited capacity for surprise, imagination, awe, wonder, amazement, beauty, goodness, peak experience, gratitude and mystery. Mystery unfolds when we stand with an open heart before God and creation, feeling deep wonder and gratitude. It is only the heart, not the mind, that can provide this rich experience of love and celebration. The more we live from the heart, the more disposed we are to imagination, wonder and peak experience.

Each of the eight Beatitudes, because they are loving attitudes, are a great gift and power in our lives, teaching us to listen to and live from our hearts. The Beatitudes empower us to make great progress in the long journey from the head to the heart, from scarcity to abundance, from 'it's hard' to 'it's an opportunity', from 'I can't' to 'I can', from blaming and complaining to acceptance, wonder, delight and gratitude. In our minds we can see life as a problem, whereas the heart relates to life as a great and wonderful mystery. Because the Beatitudes are concerned with the heart, with love, they help us to move from life as problem to life as mystery, giving us the joys of freedom, fruitfulness and fulfilment.

*Invitation: What does my heart think?*

# The Heart of Life

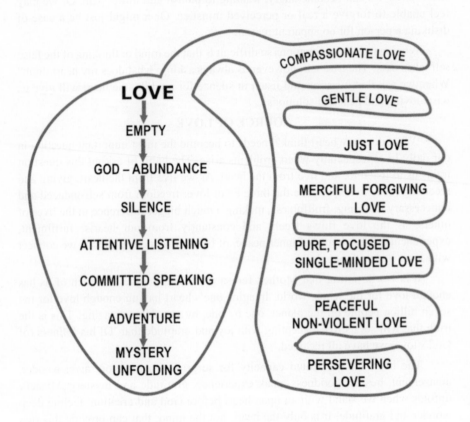

**LOVE**
↓
EMPTY
↓
GOD – ABUNDANCE
↓
SILENCE
↓
ATTENTIVE LISTENING
↓
COMMITTED SPEAKING
↓
ADVENTURE
↓
MYSTERY
UNFOLDING

COMPASSIONATE LOVE

GENTLE LOVE

JUST LOVE

MERCIFUL FORGIVING
LOVE

PURE, FOCUSED
SINGLE-MINDED LOVE

PEACEFUL
NON-VIOLENT LOVE

PERSEVERING
LOVE

We could compare the life of the Beatitudes to that of the heart, veins and arteries. We call the first Beatitude the heart because being empty for God and God's abundance is the very heart of life.

As the physical heart is full of blood, so the heart that is the first Beatitude is full of divine love. And as the physical heart needs a system of veins and arteries, so this new heart also needs a system of veins and arteries to receive God's love (veins) and to give it to the world (arteries). These veins and arteries are the other seven Beatitudes.

**Invitation:** *I open my heart and allow my love to flow.*

15

# Our Image of God

Nothing could be more important than our image of God. We need a powerful 'antibiotic' to kill the deadly infection that God is a judge who will punish us if we sin. The remedy is two-fold: we need to discover who the true God is, and then we need to experience God in a relationship of love. In the parable of the prodigal son Jesus revealed a radically new God. We see the father running to welcome his lost son, something no Jewish father would ever do, if a son squandered his inheritance. With tears of delight the father embraces his son and then celebrates. Jesus thus reveals that his heavenly Father is a God of unconditional love.

We can experience the loving God in various ways. We begin with a key line from Scripture: 'God delights in his people' *(Psalm 149:4)*. To delight is to experience extreme pleasure. Imagine Jesus in a constant state of delight, of extreme pleasure, as he enjoys the beauty and goodness he sees in each of us. What is there to do but respond with delight in return, respond to the miracle of Jesus delighting in us?

It is important that we feel delight and feel it deeply. At the moment we do so, we enter into relationship with Jesus within, which is one of mutual delight. This is the embrace of love for which our hearts long. How utterly astonishing that the relationship Jesus has with us is one of delight, and that we can respond with delight. If we could remember this great truth regularly, then our lives would be transformed.

The practice of wonder is another very effective way of experiencing the loving God. Wonder is effective because it helps us to penetrate the mystery, taking us from knowledge in the intellect to an experience of love in the heart. Delight and wonder generate each other, and gratitude follows.

We have countless opportunities to feel wonder, delight and gratitude. We think of the mercy of Jesus, forgiving each of us from the cross: 'Father, forgive them, they know not what they do' *(Luke 32:34)*. All our sins wiped out the moment we ask forgiveness! Such is the depth of his respect and appreciation for us that he tells us that we are 'the salt of the earth' and 'the light of the world' *(Matthew 5:3,14)*. Listening with the ears of the heart, we take great delight from this message that expands our faith, our hope and our capacity to love..

Nature and creation are other great sources of delight. All we need to do is to bring wonder and gratitude to the goodness, beauty, unity and truth that fill the world. We see it especially in the love, generosity and goodwill of people. Beauty and goodness mirror the presence of the loving Jesus, and the delight he takes in all creation, especially the human person. We give ourselves a great gift when we cultivate an eye for beauty and goodness, and respond by filling our day with wonder, delight and gratitude.

**Invitation:** *Jesus delights in me and in every person.*

# We Meet God in the Now

*I was regretting the past*
*and fearing the future.*
*Suddenly my Lord was speaking:*

*'My Name is I Am.'*

*He paused.*
*I waited.*

*He continued:*
*'When you live in the past*
*With its mistakes and regrets,*
*Life is hard.*
*I am not there.*

*'My name is not I WAS.*

*'When you live in the future,*
*With its problems and fears,*
*Life is hard.*
*I am not there.*

*'My name is not I WILL BE.*

*'When you live in this moment*
*Life is not hard,*
*Life is an opportunity.*

*'I am here,*
*I love you,*
*I take delight in you.*

*'I give you an abundance*
*Of what you need*
*To respond lovingly*
*To every opportunity*

*'My name is I AM.'*

# Who Am I?

Who am I, in myself, in my deepest essence? We find the answer to this great question in the first page of the Bible as we see God creating the universe by speaking it into existence. So we conclude that everyone and everything is a word of love spoken out of God's own mouth. We can add three key words to give us a fuller understanding of the human person: unique, priceless and exquisite. So we are unique, priceless and exquisite words of love spoken by God.

Evidence that we are unique or original words of love includes fingerprints and D.N.A. Scientists have been able to prove that no two snowflakes can be identical, no two of anything, no two people. Because we are all different, each of us has a unique relationship with God. Unique also means that God calls each of us to be, and to do, in a way that no other person ever could. We can only respond with wonder and gratitude to the miracle of our uniqueness.

The evidence that we are priceless words of love is to be found in the cross. Why would Christ come out of heaven to die for us if we were not priceless? Christ uses the kind of language no two lovers would ever use to convey how priceless we are: 'The hairs of your head are all numbered' *(Luke 12:7)*. The average person has between sixty and seventy thousand hairs on their head. What Christ is telling us here is that the countless details of our lives, most of them beyond our awareness, are of the utmost importance to him. How awe-inspiring!

To say that we are exquisite words of love means that we are of rare consummate excellence. Exquisite also means compelling the highest admiration. We could gain a much deeper awareness of the reality of Christ's presence simply by picturing him as he stands in front of us, in a state of delight, compelled to have the highest admiration for us. Astonishing! How can we penetrate the mystery of who we are? Only with a heart full of wonder, delight and gratitude.

We have now arrived at a very beautiful definition of who we are, as God created us, and as God always sees us. 'Who I am is a unique, priceless and exquisite word of love, spoken out of the mouth of God, for me, for you (each person I encounter in my life's journey), for those I love now and will love in the future (all the wonderful surprises Christ has in store for me), for the whole world, for the glory of God, and for the bliss of heaven.'

Understanding and appreciating ourselves in this new light is 'the truth that will set us free' to celebrate the great joys of love, freedom from all negative preoccupations and freedom to love, living a fruitful and fulfilling life.

*Invitation: Knowing who I am anchors me in Christ's love.*

# I Am Special

*(This page refers to the I of the true self)*

I'm special. In all the world there's nobody like me. Since the beginning of time, there has never been another person like me. Nobody has my smile. Nobody has my eyes, my nose, my hands, my voice. I'm special. No one can be found who has my handwriting.

Nobody anywhere has my tastes - for food or music of anything else. No one sees things just as I do. In all of time there's been no one who laughs like me, no one who cries like me. And what makes me laugh and cry will never provoke identical laughter and tears from anybody else, ever.

No one responds to any situation just as I would respond. I'm special. I'm the only one in all of creation who has my set of abilities. Oh, there will always be somebody who is better at one of the things I'm good at, but no one in the universe can reach the quality of my combination of talents, ideas, abilities and feelings.

Like a room full of musical instruments, some may excel alone, but none can match the symphony sound when all are played together. I am a symphony. Yes, a symphony!

Through all of eternity no one will ever look, talk, walk, think, be or do like me. I'm special. I'm rare. And in all rarity there is great value. Because of my great rare value, I need not attempt to imitate others. I will accept - yes, celebrate - my differences.

I'm special. And deep down I realise it's no accident that I'm special. I'm beginning to see that God made me special for a very special purpose. He has called me to be, in a way that is absolutely unique, and he has work for me that no one else can do. I am special. In all the world there is nobody like me. Nobody! I am special

## HOW SPECIAL ARE WE?

How special are we if Jesus tells us we are 'The salt of the earth and the light of the world.'? We are enormously privileged, empowered to be models, rejuvenating peoples' lives through the love and wisdom Jesus gives us in such abundance. We ponder the astonishing mystery of who we are, and the infinitely greater mystery of Jesus in us.

We can take constant encouragement from the awareness of who we are. Each morning we can look forward to the endless opportunities of the day, drawing constant strength from Jesus in us and with us. Responding with love, we bring freedom, fruitfulness and fulfillment to our own lives and the lives of others.

***Invitation:** I love the miracle of each person, so unique and so special.*

# Stunning Beauty

Psychology tells us that a healthy self-image is crucial to our well-being and behaviour. If we see ourselves in a good light, then we are likely to have a happy and successful life. We will have what it takes to deal with the difficulties that arise, responding appropriately to life as it occurs. But if we see ourselves as inferior, then our confidence and self-esteem will suffer, emotional intelligence will be low, and life will always be a burden and a struggle.

The goal is to see ourselves as God sees us, which means that we see ourselves in our God-given magnificence. The Bible and the mystics give us extremely valuable insights. Julian of Norwich, in one her revelations, lays bare the stunning beauty of the human soul.

This God-given beauty is to be found in the soul of every person, without exception. As we read Julian's passage we need to be aware that it is describing the reality of every soul, but especially one's own. 'My good Lord opened my inward eye and showed me my soul in the depth of my heart. It was as big as an endless world and like a blessed kingdom. In the middle of it sits Our Lord Jesus, God and man.

He sits in the soul in silence and peace, and he shall never leave that place where he takes in the soul, forever, as I see it. For we are his homeliest home and his dwelling place for ever. He showed me the delight he has in the human soul.'

The low awareness caused by the traumas, humiliations and hurts of life allows only a slim appreciation of the astonishing beauty of the human soul. We can, however, work towards achieving something of Julian's experience, changing the way we see ourselves, and causing our awareness, self-esteem and confidence to keep on growing.

We can start to connect with Jesus within simply by feeling wonder and astonishment, delight and gratitude, at the miracle of what Julian is telling us, line by line. To help us internalise Julian's message more easily, we make the passage personal, and put it in the present tense.

My good Lord opens my inward eye, and shows me my soul in the depth of my heart. It is as big as an endless world, and like a blessed kingdom. In the middle of my soul sits Our Lord Jesus, God and man. He sits in my soul in silence and peace, and he shall never leave that place where he takes in my soul, forever. Why? Because I am his homeliest home, and his dwelling place for ever. Jesus shows me the delight he has in me. As we respond with delight to Jesus as he delights in us, we grow into a relationship of mutual delight, of deep fulfilment, which is a foretaste of heaven.

***Invitation:*** *I say the above slowly, repeatedly, and with great delight.*

# Expanding Possibility

We have established that God is infinite love, and that the whole of humanity, person by person, is also love. Because love is our great essence or wellspring, we dare to dream of a world where nothing else but love will prevail. To ignite our dream, our passion, we need a powerful dynamic to deepen our awareness of what could be possible, what love could achieve.

We find the supreme inspiration in the promise of Christ: 'All things are possible with God.' We could apply this promise to our lives in such a way that it gives us a radically new understanding and definition of who we are. The suggestion is that we see ourselves as a constantly expanding possibility. We can be a possibility for many things, especially the following:

I am a constantly expanding possibility for:
- Responding with delight to the God who delights in us all;
- The practice of wonder and gratitude;
- The power of trust and surrender;
- The power of love, its freedom, fruitfulness and fulfilment;
- The gift of the eight loving attitudes (Beatitudes);
- Making the most of the opportunity of each moment;
- Giving each person the gift of a glad and happy heart;
- The seven gifts of wisdom, understanding, counsel, fortitude, knowledge, devotion and reverence for the sacred.
- Knowing that I can always respond with love, turning everything, no matter how difficult, into an opportunity.

Time spent pondering the gift of possibility will be extremely fruitful. Feeling wonder and gratitude, we hold the message in our hearts, surrendering, allowing it to take hold of us. This practice will ignite the flame of passion in us: 'All things are possible with God,' and therefore I am a constantly expanding possibility!

Inspired, we carry the message in our hearts, in our attitudes, and in our enthusiasm for life. In our daily interactions, our loving way of being is the spark that will ignite the flame of possibility in others. This is how we can model what it means to stand in the power of possibility.

The nature of the true self is to be dynamic, mind and heart constantly deepening and expanding. As we enter into the adventure, the pilgrimage towards our home in heaven, our awareness and the love in our hearts, are always deepening and expanding. The paradox is that the more we can surrender, be aware and be love, the more we deepen and expand. Attitudes are transformed as our minds and hearts constantly expand with endless possibility.

***Invitation:*** *I live in the joy of being an expanding possibility.*

# From Possibility to Reality

When we feel inspired by a vision of what is possible, we cannot wait to step into the reality. The miracle is that we already have the reality, for 'We are in Christ and Christ is in us.' With the reality of his presence, we automatically have the abundance of his love, 'The spring of living water.' So we need to accept, to trust and to surrender, allowing what is, the presence of Christ, and the abundance of his life, to be the great reality in our awareness..

Anyone who is committed to the spiritual journey is constantly growing in wisdom and love. The enlarging boxes of the above diagram illustrate this gradual deepening and expansion. The arrows represent the infinity of God's love, the pull of which is enlarging our minds and hearts in the direction of infinity. We cooperate with the healing action of the Holy Spirit in us. The wonder of so great a mystery! So stunning, overflowing with joy and peak experience.Our minds and our hearts keep on expanding, moving us from possibility to reality, from belief in our minds to the inner knowing of the heart. In one sense we have arrived, but in another sense we are always arriving, because our awareness is always expanding.

***Invitation:*** *My heart delights in the expanding power of God's love.*

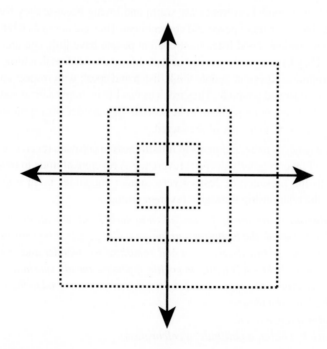

# Reverence, Going Deeper

When we live from our centre, the place of deep love, our true self, we bring an attitude of reverence to the whole of life: reverence for the infinite sacredness of God, reverence for the sacredness of self and of others, and reverence for God's creation in all its beauty and goodness. We also need to include reverence for the gift of time and the present moment that contains the wealth of God's abundant gifts.

Reverence is an attitude, a response, of the heart, to what is sacred. Reverence includes deep respect for the sacred, sorrow for our wrong-doing, humility and love, wonder and gratitude. We say that God is sacred because God is holy, full of goodness and love. The human soul is also sacred because it mirrors the sacredness of God. And creation is sacred because it is penetrated through and through by the energy of God's presence and God's love.

The sacred requires a response of deep reverence, the practice of which connects us to our core, to the sacredness of our true self, to Jesus within, to the sacred in each person, and to the sacredness of creation. The experience can sometimes be a peak experience of deep love, union and peace. The practice of reverence engages the whole person, mind, feelings, body and spirit. It promotes wholeness and well-being, and integrates us at the deepest level.

Those who model reverence are warm and loving because they live from the heart. They have an aura of peace and contentment. They are not rushed but have time, making them patient, good listeners. Reverent people have little ego and are rich in humanity. They have a gentleness that accepts life, and a wisdom that turns difficulties into opportunities. Reverent people think, listen and speak with respect and humility, with love, wonder and gratitude. They teach us that life is simply a great and wonderful mystery to be lived, not a problem to be solved. They model what it means to live in the present moment, in the joy of the sacred.

Our day needs many moments of mindfulness to cultivate reverence. Doing the Abundance Prayer regularly deepens reverence. A reverent attitude to time makes us attentive to the presence of Jesus Every human encounter is an opportunity to transform the relationship through a reverent attitude.

*Invitation: I slow down! I pause often to make brief acts of reverence to God, and to the good, the beautiful and the sacred in people. I bow my head a little, very slowly, feeling deep respect and humility, love, wonder and gratitude. I do this also with the special gifts in my life, my home, the air, sunshine, food, water, etc., creation. I bring an attitude of reverence for the sacred to the whole of life with all its abundance.*
*I feel reverence often.*
*I make it a habit, an attitude, a celebration.*

# The Prayer of Abundance

Could we imagine ourselves taking responsibility for the world, for the six and a half billion people, and for all the massive problems on the planet? We could dismiss this idea as fantasy, or as an impossible burden. We see a massive opportunity, however, when we remember that each of us has 'The spring of living water', the infinity of God's love, in us. So why not open our hearts, and allow the ocean of love in us to flow out to everyone the world over, in an endless current of rejuvenation and transformation? We find a simple and easy method of allowing the love to flow in what we call the Prayer of Abundance.

## THE METHOD

Welcome to the prayer that makes our lives abundant. We begin: elbows by our sides, we point our fingers out to the sides. The left hand represents the negative beliefs of the past: I'm not good enough, it's hard, I can't, etc. The right hand represents the negative feelings we have about the future: fear, worry and anxiety. These negatives influences are our far country, the same far country where the prodigal son found himself.

Like him we waste our gifts, our time and our life. As the prodigal came to his senses, we also need to waken up, aware that we have a choice, that we can return from our far country, the negative world of fear and scarcity, of blaming and complaining, to the Father's house, the place of abundance which is our home.

So we move our hands towards each other, towards home, into the present, the now, where God, our Father is waiting to welcome us with a love greater than we could ever imagine. We join our hands. We feel the embrace of the Father's love. We feel it especially in our hands. Now we use it. With the backs of our hands we push out all the influences that trouble us, fear, worry, anxiety, guilt, blaming, complaining etc.

As we push out, we're creating sacred space to enter into a deep and intimate relationship with the loving God within. Space also to receive life in abundance from the generous God. We feel wonder and gratitude as we bring our hands down, resting them on our lap, palms facing each other directly. We relax our fingers, we drop our thumbs. We close our eyes gently, if that is comfortable. We stay very still and focused.

We picture the radiant light of Jesus, brighter than the sun, surrounding us and filling us. We relax into this heavenly light, protecting us and healing us. We feel the loving energy of Jesus flowing through our body, our mind and our feelings. As it flows it heals us deeply, heals us at the core of our being. We listen to Jesus in the intimacy of our heart as he tells us: I love you more than you could ever imagine. We allow these words to touch us deeply: I love you more than you could ever imagine. Feeling deep wonder and gratitude we pray: I thank you, Lord, for the wonder of my being and the miracle of your presence in me. We feel wonder, we feel gratitude.

We have created sacred space for the love in our hearts to flow freely out through our hands to those we want to pray for, sacred space also for Jesus to do what is necessary in their lives. We hold those we love and anyone else we want to pray for in our sacred space. We picture the light around them. We feel the love flowing freely out through our hands to them. We let go and allow Jesus to take over. We feel wonder and gratitude, in the heart.

We hold anyone we find difficult or anyone who has hurt us in our sacred space, picturing the light around them. We feel the love flowing freely out through our hands to them. We allow Jesus to take over, feeling wonder and gratitude. We thank you Lord for the wonder of their being, and the miracle of your presence in them. Holding the planet earth in our sacred space we surround it and fill it with the radiant light of Jesus. We feel his loving energy flowing freely from our heart out through our hands to everyone and everything, to all the great needs of the world, and all the poverty and hunger, all the injustice and oppression, all the wars and their terrible consequences. All the sickness, grief and suffering.

As we pray the Abundance Prayer we become one with Jesus in us in his great compassion for the world and in his great prayer for the world. What a gift, what a privilege. Let us feel inspired, deeply inspired. We thank you, for the wonder of their being and the miracle of your presence in them. (Visit www.theabundanceprayer.com for a free download of the CD).

## SHORTER FORM

We bring our hands together, joined. We feel the embrace of God's love. We use this love to push out all negative influences, fear, worry, etc. We hold in our sacred space any person(s) or situation(s) we want to pray for. We put the radiant light of Jesus around them. We allow the love to flow freely from our hearts, out through our hands to them. We allow Jesus to do what is necessary. Feeling wonder and gratitude we pray: I thank you, Lord, for the wonder of their being and the miracle of your presence in them.

## THE ABUNDANCE PRAYER AND THE EUCHARIST

We could say that Jesus was doing the Abundance Prayer on the cross. With arms outstretched he embraced the whole human race, and his love flowed in infinite abundance from his heart to each and every person. Jesus continues this prayer in the celebration of the Eucharist. He is the priest and the celebrant is standing in his shoes at one with him in his prayer. Each member of the congregation is also invited to stand in the shoes of Jesus, at one with him and the celebrant. Jesus is thus fulfilling his promise to draw all people into his kingdom. How very privileged we are.

To download a free copy of the Abundance Prayer and seven other meditations, go to www.youtube.com/visionbeinspired

25

# *Allowing!*

The Abundance Prayer consists of

Letting Go

Surrendering

Creating Sacred Space

Allowing your love to flow

Allowing Jesus to take over and do what is

necessary.

Allowing!

Allowing!

Allowing!

# An Approach to Meditation

To meditate, it is helpful to use a mantra or sacred sound, preferably the Holy Name which has great significance. When the soldiers came to arrest Jesus they asked him his name. As he pronounced it the soldiers fell to the ground, such was the power of the Holy Name.

When Peter and John were going into the temple, a cripple asked for alms. 'Silver and gold I haven't got' said Peter, 'but what I have, I give you: in the name of Jesus, get up and walk' (Acts: 3:8). Instantly the man sprang to his feet completely healed. What we need to appreciate is that when we pronounce the Holy Name with faith, love and reverence, then, like the Apostles, we make the risen Jesus present. Miracles happen!

John Main, Benedictine, who has had such world-wide success in getting people to meditate, encouraged the use of the mantra, Maranatha, meaning, come Lord Jesus. Main recommended this Aramaic word because a mantra in another language would be less likely to remind one of something else, in this way reducing the level of distractions during meditation.

It is helpful to prepare for meditation by doing a brief version of the Abundance Prayer because of the sacred space the prayer creates. Good posture is important as it helps us to concentrate better, and to create a sacred mood. So we sit upright, eyes gently closed, feeling comfortable, very still, relaxed. We smile gently, breathe slowly, feel good, happy that Jesus is intimately present in us and with us.

We now extend the Holy Name over the length of our breath as we inhale and again as we exhale. As we do so we feel wonder and gratitude at the miracle that is taking place. Jesus in us is loving and transforming us and all the world. The more we surrender and allow the Holy Name, Jesus, or Maranatha, to say itself in us, the more effective our meditation becomes.

This practice expands our sacred space, generating more and more love in us and around us. We become fields of loving energy, more abundant, for ourselves and for the world. Regular practice of meditation, increasing the flow of love in us, helps us greatly to live each of the Beatitudes more fully. It is recommended that we meditate for twenty minutes, morning and evening.

Everyone who meditates has to deal with distractions. The bad news is that they get worse as we get older, as our powers of concentration wane. The good news is that distractions do not diminish the effectiveness of our meditation. This depends on the intention to surrender our hearts to Jesus and the action of the Holy Spirit in us. So we give distractions no attention, treating them like the traffic on the street. Whenever we notice a distraction, we come back gently to saying the mantra.

*Invitation:* Daily meditation: what a power, what a gift!

# The Abundance Prayer, Meditation and Community

When we create sacred space in the Abundance Prayer and continue into meditation, letting go and surrendering, we connect with the life of the Blessed Trinity, Father, Son and Holy Spirit. In the silence and stillness we keep going deeper, and in this process of love the bonds of love establish and grow stronger. We experience a belonging to the divine community of love which is the indwelling Trinity.

By simply holding the human race in our sacred space, allowing our love to flow and the Holy Spirit to act, we are co-creating a world-wide community. This community of love includes every person, with the Trinity its source and centre. Meditation thus engages us in an action that brings about the unity of the human race for which Christ prayed: 'That they may all be one' *(John 17:21)*.

Meditation is the very essence of spiritual practice because it generates a love that is pure (absence of ego-driven agendas) and undiluted. Saints owe their integrity and influence for good to the purity of their love. That is why it is so essential for the individual person to commit to daily meditation, and for groups to meditate weekly, if possible. Groups can preferably include other faiths or those of no faith. It is now generally recognised in Asia that the basic communities of that region need to be inter-faith communities.

We find the model community for the transformation of the world in the Acts of the Apostles. It begins with the Holy Spirit descending on the apostles who are transformed by the power of divine love, a love that unites them as one: 'They were all of one mind and heart' *(Acts of the Apostles 4:32)*. They then sold what they had and shared with one another. Goods were distributed to the members of the group. Every person's need was looked after, especially the needs of the poor, the sick, widows, orphans, etc. Here we have a perfect example of the meaning of justice: the needs of each person were attended to with the utmost compassion.

Small groups, practicing meditation and living lives committed to the practice of justice and peace, have a hugely significant role to play in the future of the world. These communities of love, focusing on the fundamental human values of compassion, justice and community, bring about the change everyone needs, which is the reign of God, the kingdom of God on earth.

*Invitation:* I can give myself the priceless gift of daily meditation.

# The Use of the Breath

Using the breath is another very effective way of meditating. Wonder, reverence and gratitude, essential attitudes for meditation, will deepen when we appreciate the rich meaning the Bible gives the breath. In the Old Testament, the Hebrews had deep reverence for the gift of their breathing. They saw it as very sacred because they understood it as God's way of sharing his own life with them. And so we have the expression, 'the breath of life'. The Hebrews saw death as God taking away their breath.

In the New Testament the breath had even greater significance. We see Jesus breathing on the apostles inviting them to 'Receive the Holy Spirit'. So the Spirit came to them in the form of a breath. This means that we can be aware of the Spirit coming to us, and living in us through every breath that we take.

We can begin to meditate with the breath by using the Abundance Prayer for a short time to create silence, stillness and sacred space, and to become aware of Jesus and his Spirit in us. We now begin to observe our breath. We bring a sense of wonder and gratitude to the miracle of what it is: a most extraordinary mystery, the means through which God is sharing divine life with us. We observe how gentle our breath is, profoundly gentle. The gentleness of our breath reminds us of the presence of the gentle Christ and the gentle Spirit in us. We take time to ponder this great mystery.

We also notice how intimate our breath is, probably the most intimate thing to us. This intimacy reminds us of the intimacy of the gentle Christ in us. We continue to focus on our breathing, its extraordinary meaning and the power it has to give us a direct experience of the gentle Christ and his Spirit. We keep bringing awe and wonder, delight and gratitude, to what is happening. The more we surrender to our breathing, to Christ, and to the gentle action of the Spirit in us, the more we are healed of the wounds we carry, nourished in our desire for God, and transformed and integrated at every level.

We can also use our breathing to help others. When we see any person in a state of distress, upset or pain, we can breathe out the love of Jesus to them, allowing the Holy Spirit to heal and transform their hearts. We can also include a family, a group, a country or the world in this practice.

Using our breath in this way is a simple but deep and effective prayer, and has many benefits. It improves our awareness, our mindfulness, helping us to live in the present moment. It causes the love in our hearts to flow to others and their needs, making our lives more fruitful. And it can be used for a few moments or longer at any time.

*Invitation:* I can make my breathing a great power of love.

# Befriend the Cross
# as the Cross Befriends You

We look at the Cross and ponder … and ponder … and ponder.

We look at the Cross and allow it to speak to us.

We put aside our thinking mind, and just be:

silent and still before this awesome mystery of love.

With extended arms Jesus embraces the whole human race.

His heart wide open, his love flows,

flows with infinity and for eternity to every person.

The silent and compelling invitation of Jesus from the Cross:

Open your mind and your heart, open your whole being.

Allow yourself to be touched as never before.

Your sins are but a puff of smoke in a great wind

when sorrow fills your heart.

Allow the flow of my love to heal and comfort you,

to strengthen and inspire you.

Open your heart and allow yourself to be filled to overflowing

with my countless gifts,

with patience, patience, and yet more patience

towards life as it comes, and people as they are.

Be free to love, and love, with a never-ending love.

Allow your life to be a joyous celebration of my blessings.

Befriend the Cross as the Cross befriends you,

and you will know that 'all will be well, and all will be well,

And all manner of thing will be well.'

# Our Travelling Companions

Isn't it astonishing? Abundance is our birthright because the generous God has ordained it so. Christ came to give us plenty of everything we need in every area of our life. We can only conclude that a wonderfully fulfilling-life is available to us. The right tools are all-important. Rather than awakening to the worries and burdens of another day, we can choose to awaken to two travelling companions that will revolutionise our lives. These new friends are the gifts of wonder and gratitude, the regular practice of which will give us a truly abundant life.

When we feel wonder and gratitude we secrete endorphins, the natural morphine of the body, into the system. Endorphins strengthen our immune system, give us greater emotional strength, deepen our peace, and our love of life. Mother Teresa inspired a large group of students at Harvard university with such wonder and gratitude that their immunoglobulin levels rose sharply. These levels were measured before and after the lecture. We learn from this evidence that we can achieve extraordinary results by simply practising wonder and gratitude. We will be stronger and healthier, have better relationships, and be more resilient and inspired.

The practice of using our travelling companions gives us the extraordinary benefits of the three Fs of love: freedom, fruitfulness and fulfilment. By healing our hurts, and by dissolving the fear, worry and anxiety that cause us to turn in on ourselves, wonder and gratitude set us free, the first F of love. Our hearts open and God's abundant love in us flows freely and effortlessly. Generosity becomes automatic as we respond with ease to peoples' needs, the second F of love.

Our experience of loving service makes us fulfilled, the third F of love. Fulfilment is simply a deep contentment, which is an experience of Christ's gift of inner peace. Generosity can often make major demands on us, especially with people we find difficult. The release of endorphins, triggered by the practice of wonder and gratitude, helps us greatly in our efforts to love, as we become more free, fruitful and fulfilled.

Our new freedom helps us to look out from ourselves, more aware of the beauty and goodness everywhere. Our attitudes change wonderfully. We see that life is a continual conveyor belt of gifts, a non-stop miracle, and we are often overwhelmed with wonder and gratitude.

We conclude that the practice of these gifts is the beating heart of the person who is vibrant and inspired, engaged in making the world a better place. Constantly empowered by our travelling companions, we awaken our sleeping giant, the unlimited power of God's love in us. The adventure of life opens up and we journey into the mystery that constantly unfolds in surprise and discovery.

***Invitation:*** *I delight in my travelling companions.*

# Wonder: A Priceless Gift

We have seen how we humans are most precious words of love spoken by the God of love. The writer of the psalms responded in wonder and gratitude to this great mystery: 'I thank you, Lord, for the wonder of my being' (Psalm 138:14). Wonder is a most delightful experience. We see it in the eyes of a child, alive with excitement, as it explores and discovers. Wonder will do the same for us, when we make it a constant practice, unfolding the endless world of mystery, for which the heart hungers.

Wonder is a response of the heart to an experience of beauty or goodness that resonates deeply. We can experience wonder by bringing an open, feeling heart to beauty or goodness, or to life or creation. Deeply touched, we allow wonder to arise in us spontaneously with a knowing or experience of God's loving presence, and of the joys of creation. We stand spellbound, stunned by the mystery unfolding before our very eyes.

Wonder engages the whole person, filling us with delight, and gratitude. The experience of beauty and goodness is what triggers wonder. That is why we need to keep awakening to the beauty of human beings and of creation, awakening also to the goodness in each person. Awakening to the signs of God's presence, and to the mystery of life as it occurs.

Wonder gives us a direct and immediate experience of God because God is beauty, goodness and mystery, and God is love and truth. Wonder also gives us a sense of the sacred, disposing us to feel reverence for the infinite sacredness of God, the sacredness of self, each person, and creation.

The child, eyes alive with wonder, is our greatest model. Artists, poets, saints and mystics are also great models, forever inspiring us. 'When it's all over, I want to say: all my life I was a bride married to amazement (wonder), and the bridegroom taking the world into my arms.' - Mary Oliver, poet.

When our lives are underpinned by the habit of wonder, everything falls into place. We grow in the wonder of self, the wonder of the Creator and of everyone and everything. We engage more deeply with the mystery of life. Love flows more freely, and life has great meaning. Wonder is truly miraculous. Dissolving the influences that suppress us, it takes us effortlessly into the world of abundance.

Wonder is an absolute joy and delight, a most essential gift to give to both oneself and the world. People cry out for those who will model what it means to be alive and vibrant, in love with life, and with all that is good and beautiful. Nothing awakens or inspires us like a child or an adult in a state of wonder. How privileged we are to be able to model wonder for others.

***Invitation:*** *I thank God often for the wonder of everyone and everything.*

# Gratitude: Happiness Achieved

The happiest people are those who are most grateful, even for the simplest things. Gratitude is a loving, enthusiastic response to the giver of a gift. Life is one continual conveyor belt of gifts. How aware are we? If we were fully aware we would recognise how privileged we are, and would be overwhelmed with wonder, appreciation, gratitude and peak experience.

We would constantly thank God for the wonder of everyone and everything, and for the miracle of God's loving presence, manifested in all the beauty and goodness around us. Life would be so very inspiring and gratitude would be automatic. How do we achieve the habit of being grateful? By being awake and aware. Gratitude requires the effort of a thinking, wakeful mind. We cannot be truly grateful until we awaken and recognise how everything is gift, and how utterly dependent and interdependent we all are.

The whole universe is a gift, mother earth, the air we breathe, sunshine, light, water, food and sleep. The mind and each organ in the body is a most astonishing gift. And we are reminded of the greatest of all gifts, which is the love we receive from God and from countless people. With constant and enthusiastic practice gratitude becomes automatic in everyday life. The practice of gratitude has great power, moving us to a rich experience of nature and creation, and of what is great in life and in people. Instead of complaining about what we do not have, we thank God for what we do have. This practice expands our hearts with more than enough of everything we need. Aware of being so privileged, and of everything being a gift, gratitude follows automatically, giving us a glad and happy heart.

Gratitude is miraculous, inspiring us to give generously. A grateful heart is a gentle heart, just, respectful, reverent, patient and kind. A grateful heart is a big stand for the world and for all that is best in the life of every person.

A grateful heart takes no one or nothing for granted, but is always helpful, hospitable and welcoming. A grateful heart gives us a new awareness, and a deep experience of the three Fs of love. We experience ourselves as free, free to be oneself rather than to have to conform. We respond more easily in love to others, and we are more at ease with ourselves and the world. We are also more contented, more fulfilled.

The practice of gratitude changes our relationship to everyone and everything. Gratitude towards any person breaks down the barriers of dislike, prejudice, anger and vengeance, taking us to a place of acceptance and compassion. And so the practice of gratitude promotes mental health, general well-being and good relationships. When we are grateful for material things, we move from the prison of attachment, greed and possessiveness to the freedom and joy of respect and appreciation for God's unlimited gifts.

***Invitation:*** *On awakening, I say thank you, I finish at bedtime.*

33

# The Gift of a Smile

God gives each of us extraordinary gifts, the use of which enables us to grow into a fuller and more rounded humanity, a deeper maturity and responsibility, and a freedom expressed in our love for life and compassion for people. When we neglect our gifts we struggle and underachieve. It is amazing, however, the difference something as simple as a frequent smile can make.

What's in a smile? Research shows that smiling has numerous benefits for health and well-being. A thirty year study looked at the smiles of students from old college photos. Having measured the success and well- being of each student, the study showed that those with the widest smiles had the most long-lasting marriages. They also ranked highest in the areas of well-being and happiness, and in their loving service of others.

Other research shows that smiling makes us healthier, reducing the hormone levels that cause stress, including adrenaline, dopamine and cortisol, and increasing endorphins and serotonin, which are the mood and health enhancing hormones. Smiling is also much less demanding than frowning, requiring only seventeen muscles, while frowning needs forty three. Only one adult in three smiles more than twenty times a day while children smile four hundred times daily.

Smiling also enhances our relationships and our prayer. Like wonder, a smile awakens the love in our hearts. A smile is the beginning of wonder, disposing us to see beauty and goodness. A smile welcomes, makes us approachable and communicates gentle love. The listening ear, the kind word and the smile that comes from the heart, are the lifeblood of loving relationships. A smile says: I accept you, I appreciate you, I love you. A little smile as we pray helps us to pray from the heart, with love. We can smile often as we feel the wonder of our being and the miracle of Jesus in us.

Ideally we would smile like the child, continually. Is this possible if we are in pain or difficulty or darkness? We have many examples of people who smile in such situations. Mother Teresa had no feeling of God's presence for almost fifty years. Even in her darkness she lived a life of unshakable faith and total commitment, and she greeted every one with a smile that came from her heart. Here we have an example of how Jesus sometimes deprives us of the experience of his love and his presence in order to lead us to a deeper, more mature faith.

Edith Stein, philosopher, now St. Teresa Benedicta, was a German Jew who converted to Catholicism, and became a Carmelite nun. The Nazis entered her convent in their hunt for Jews, and lined up the nuns, one of whom observed that Sr. Teresa stood out from the other sisters. Her faint smile communicated an inner peace, and an acceptance of her impending death.

***Invitation:*** *I enrich myself and others with a smile, all day long.*

# The Gift of Peak Experience

When Carl Jung was asked if he believed in God, he replied, 'No, I don't believe, I know.' How could Jung respond with total certainty? He had an experience of being loved by God, what is called a 'peak experience'. Peak experience takes our faith from belief in one's mind to a knowing in the heart, giving us what is called a living faith. The child is our model. Christ told us that unless we become like the child we cannot enter God's kingdom, the world of peak experience.

A peak experience occurs when we are so overwhelmed by God's generosity and beauty that we are filled with bliss, delight and gratitude. We are taken out of ourselves and beyond ourselves, entering into the mystery of God's love. At that moment all our desires are fulfilled beyond anything we could ever have dreamed. Life has become the dance or celebration Christ intends it to be.

A peak experience is a most exquisite gift through which God is telling us: 'I love you, I'm present in you and with you.' The past and future disappear. Time stands still in the now. We feel integrated, whole and complete, at peace with self, God, others and with life. The trigger could be a sunset, a view from a mountaintop, or an experience of intimacy, or it could be an occasion of great suffering or grief when God reveals his intimate presence to comfort and strengthen us.

A peak experience makes us aware of the interconnectedness of all God's creation, giving us a sense of belonging in the universe, at one with God and the true self in each person. We experience ourselves as living branches of the vine: 'I am the vine, you are the branches.'

Abraham Maslow, the psychologist, says that everyone has peak experiences, but most people do not recognise them. Unfortunately there is no cultural acceptance of them, nor has religion recognised them, with the exception of saints and mystics. The Desert Fathers in the early Church, however, put great emphasis on these experiences, encouraging people to relive them. By doing so, they said, we could connect up all our peaks, creating a plateau or higher level of awareness that would become permanent with practice.

We can distinguish three different kinds of peak experience. First, there are the ones God gives us - when it pleases God. The more empty we are of selfish (false self) preoccupations and attachments, the more we create the sacred space for God to surprise and astonish us. It happens when we least expect it.

We can generate peak experience for others by surprising them with acts of generosity, listening with love and speaking words of praise and encouragement. The element of surprise is what makes a loving act a peak experience for another person.

We can create peak experience for ourselves by opening our eyes in wonder and gratitude to the infinite variety and beauty of God's creation. The regular use of our travelling companions, wonder and gratitude, as we discover the divine beauty and goodness anew each day, give us a life rich in peak experience as the world of mystery unfolds continually.

We can, for instance, create a peak experience first thing in the morning by bringing wonder and gratitude to the miracle of wakening up alive. We allow our eyes to open wide, our face to break into a broad smile, and we feel delight at this great gift of God. We can often focus on some object of beauty or goodness that holds special significance for us, a flower, a landscape, etc. Or we can observe the love and generosity in another person. We give ourselves a peak experience by feeling wonder and gratitude at the miracle we see..

Small children are outstanding teachers. Their eyes are alive with wonder as they explore and discover, constantly creating peak experiences for themselves, and for those who observe them. Children teach us to live in the present moment, making life an adventure. They teach us to respond in wonder to the miracle of each moment, creating peak experiences for ourselves and for others, and open to the peak experiences God desires to give us.

When we seek peak experience for itself it will always elude us. That is why attitudes of humility, generosity, wonder and gratitude are so fundamental. We can learn from, and be inspired by those who have great hardships and suffering, and yet bring generosity, joy and gratitude, constant peak experience, to their lives. A woman in a wheelchair: 'I never cease to wonder at the miracle of my eyes, ears and hands, every organ in my body, and especially the legs of others.' The poor of the Third World are wonderful models, always inspiring us by their acceptance of what cannot be changed, and by the generosity of their lives.

Life is one continuous opportunity that raises our awareness when we respond to it. By making life a dance or celebration we bring peak experience to our own lives and to those of others, as well as creating the sacred space for God to surprise us with peak experience. The gifts of God are so mysterious, so exquisite, so astonishing, so miraculous, so full of the stuff of peak experience that is always new. Wonder is the key. It is no surprise, therefore, that the psalm encourages us to make wonder a constant practice. 'Serve the Lord with awe and wonder.' Awareness of the endless beauty and goodness that surround us is what will awaken wonder.

Frequent peak experiences, causing the love in us to flow so freely, are hugely beneficial to our growth in awareness, to our well-being, to our success, and to deepening attitudes of love and compassion towards the whole human race, person by person.

*Invitation: I create peak experiences for myself and for others.*

# Beauty and its Delights

Beauty is the smiling face of God,

delighting in us and in creation.

The smiling face of God ... actually delighting in us ...

How miraculous!   How delightful!   What perfect joy!

How grateful can we be for the wonder of so much beauty?

And for the miracle of God's face, hidden in all beauty?

Because beauty is everywhere, the God of delight is everywhere,

always smiling, and through that smile,

inviting us into a relationship of

Mutual Love ..... and Delight ..... and Peak Experience .....

What we need, and urgently, is the grace of a deeper awareness:

an awareness full of the appreciation of beauty;

an awareness that recognises the smiling face of God

in all beauty.

Beauty always inviting.

Beauty always delighting.

Beauty always new.

Beauty, the smiling face of God, delighting in us and in creation.

Open our eyes, Lord, to the beauty that is everywhere,

especially the inner beauty in each person.

*May we see your smiling face in all beauty,*

*delighting in us and in every person.*

*Lord, help us to delight in you as you delight in us.*

# Eucharist and Celebration

The celebration of the Eucharist is a deeply loving encounter with the risen Jesus. As we embrace the new lifestyle, outlined in this book, we discover that the Mass is so very enriching, full of opportunities for celebration and peak experience. We need to be clear that the Mass is about mystery, and that Jesus is inviting us to enter into the mystery, for which he has given us the key gifts of wonder, gratitude and reverence. Jesus is the priest who celebrates the Eucharist. He extends an extraordinary privilege to the celebrant and the congregation, inviting each one to stand in his shoes, at one with him in bringing his compassion to the world.

When we speak of the presence of Jesus in the Mass, we mean that He is present in four very special and dynamic ways. He is present in the priest by virtue of his ordination, and also present in the congregation: 'Where two or three are gathered in my name, there am I in their midst.' He is present in the readings as the word of God is proclaimed, and he is present in the gift of communion. We need to stand back in wonder and gratitude, astonished at the privilege of being touched by Jesus in each of these four very intimate and sacred ways.

A key moment arises at the beginning of the celebration when we are invited to call to mind our sins. This is an opportunity to experience the Father's mercy, enabling us to be more fully at one with Jesus during the celebration, in bringing his mercy and compassion to the entire world.

When we are present with a listening heart, we are healed, nourished and inspired by the prayers of the Mass, and especially by the word of God in the readings. Our attitudes are changed, and our hearts expanded as we bring wonder and gratitude to this extraordinary gift of God speaking so intimately to us. The focus and sacred space we create allows the Holy Spirit to draw us deep into the mystery of God's love. This can be a profound peak experience.

We are one with Jesus in offering the infinite merits of his life, death and resurrection to the Father, represented by the offering of the bread and wine. With Jesus and the celebrant we also offer our own love and suffering, and that of the world, to the glory of the Father, and for the salvation of the world. The words of consecration transform the bread and wine into the living presence of Jesus. At communion we receive Jesus, 'the Bread of Life'. Entering into deep union with him, he teaches us to love unconditionally, giving ourselves in loving service to others.

The final words of the Mass tell us to 'Go in peace to love and serve the Lord,' which means that we love and serve others as Jesus did. Jesus empowers us to accept, encourage and support people, and to help them in their needs. At one with Jesus, in the immensity of his compassion for the world, we draw people into God's kingdom of love, justice and peace.

*Invitation: The Eucharist is an astonishing privilege and gift.*

# The Gift of Hospitality

Of all God's gifts, hospitality is one of the greatest. To be hospitable is to be warm and generous, kind and friendly, in welcoming a stranger or a guest. The greatness of hospitality lies in its power to open the door of both one's heart and one's home. We welcome people, making them feel wanted and appreciated, and giving them a sense of belonging. The experience of hospitality nourishes and renews both the giver and the receiver, in mind and heart, in soul and body.

If we stop to ponder the mystery of creation, especially mother earth, we can be overwhelmed by how lavish God's hospitality is towards the human race. The planet earth is truly a garden of Eden, overflowing with everything we need. The Bible is the story of God's hospitality which we see mirrored in the extraordinary generosity of Abraham. When he saw three strangers approaching he ran to welcome them, bowing low in reverence *(Genesis 18:2)*. Then he and Sarah prepared a great banquet for their guests.

Following Abraham's example, reverence for the guest or the stranger became an intrinsic part of Jewish culture. In African tradition a stranger is a source of blessing: 'Let the stranger come so that the people may prosper.' (African proverb). In earlier times people left their doors open in case a stranger needed shelter. At Christmas there was the tradition of candles lighting in the windows to welcome Mary and Joseph, the fire was bedded down, and milk was left on the table for the new born.

A family stood on the street watching their house burn down when a passer-by stopped to express regret. A twelve year old responded: 'we do have a home but now we have no place to put it.' How extraordinary that one so young would see that a home is about hospitality and loving relationships. The difference between a house and a home illustrates this great truth. A house consists of walls, doors, etc., and becomes a home only when the occupants have loving, hospitable attitudes. We are without a lasting home on this earth, for we are pilgrims and strangers here. Jesus has shown us the ultimate hospitality by preparing an eternal home for us, a home that is a heaven of blissful fulfilment.

With the greatest tenderness and compassion Jesus opens his heart to us in hospitality: 'Come to me all you who labour and are overburdened and I will give you rest.' In another place he invites us to a relationship of mutual hospitality: 'Make your home in me as I make mine in you.' In the celebration of the Eucharist we experience this two-way hospitality: we welcome Jesus and Jesus welcomes us. He challenges us to extend hospitality to others: 'I was hungry and you fed me ... I was sick and in prison and you visited me.' The disciples who met Jesus on the road to Emmaus recognised him only when they offered him hospitality.

*Invitation: Lord, may my heart overflow with hospitality.*

# Our Language, Our Life

Life is essentially a conversation and conversation consists of listening and speaking. The choice is to listen and speak with the true self or to do so with the false self. To listen with the true self is to listen for possibility, for the good, to listen for what God can do, and for what love can do. We can also listen with the wisdom that wants to turn the difficulties of life into opportunities. This listening transforms our attitudes, our language and our life, causing us to speak words that are encouraging, generous and life-giving.

If we are not listening with the true self, then it is the false self that is doing our listening, focusing on scarcity, fear, worry, etc. This listening, frozen by negative preoccupations, gives us a very bleak and miserable outlook. It causes us to react often with words of anger, blame, impatience etc. The language we use is critical because we create the life that we have through our language. We are what we say, and what we say is given by the particular listening that we choose to adopt. If we speak negatively, then we pollute ourselves and our environment. We suffer and everyone else suffers.

The listening ear and the kind word are the first tools in the kit-bag of the hospitable person. The language of love, caused by the listening of the true self, activates God's love, 'the spring of living water', in us, making it flow powerfully. The benefits are enormous: good communication, improved relationships, cooperation, a sense of belonging, self-esteem and confidence enhanced, well-being improved, people valued and cared for, and a loving relationship with God.

It is a principle of life that we always attract what we speak. Speak abundance and abundance flows to us, and we will always have what we need and more. Generous, helpful people will cross our path. However, if we think and speak scarcity, then we will always be poor and miserable. We will attract, and be attracted to, people like ourselves. Language largely determines our well-being. Negative language poisons the mind, the emotions and the body. Loving, grateful language, however, promotes the wellness of the whole person.

A woman had twelve operations in the last ten years. Yet she looks really well, and lives a full life. Her wellness is due largely to her loving attitudes and language. She inspired herself and those around her with her language of trust, hope and gratitude. We need to cultivate the language of abundance: 'I can', 'God is with me', 'God gives me what I need', 'all will be well', 'I always thank God', 'I don't worry', 'I trust in God', 'I'm always looked after', etc. The language that listens and speaks love, has unlimited power to transform our lives and the lives of others, giving us the joys of freedom, fruitfulness and fulfilment.

*Invitation: I keep speaking the language of love and gratitude.*

# Listening With Love

Chinese culture had three symbols for listening: the heart, the eyes and the ears. The heart is all-important because it is love that gives listening its power to connect with people, establishing and deepening relationship. To listen with the heart is to listen with a warm interest in the other person. We listen for who they are, a unique and priceless word of love spoken by God. We listen also for the gift, the loving influence, they are for oneself and for others. We respond with wonder and gratitude to the privilege of their love and support.

If we sense a need, we listen with sensitivity and patience for their pain or anger or struggle, or for their insecurity or confusion. This listening is extremely influential because it opens the heart, allowing the love in us to flow to the other who then feels accepted and loved, comforted and supported.

Healing takes place, confidence grows, and the well-being necessary for a normal life starts to be restored. We resist the temptation to give advice, aware that it not only stops the flow of love, but it also prevents the person from resolving things for themselves.

To listen with the eyes, the second symbol, is to have no fear of eye contact, giving the other person one's full attention. A mother reported how her relationship with her children improved greatly when she listened. She simply stopped and made eye contact whenever one of them wished to speak to her.

To listen with the ears, the third symbol, is not only to listen to what is said, but also to listen to what is not said, to what the other person may not even be aware of. This listening engages the intuition, which is a knowing without knowing why. Intuition is that place in us where the Holy Spirit and the true self are one, telling us when to be silent, when to speak, what to say and what to do. The insights gained through intuition, giving us a deeper understanding and compassion, enable us to be of much greater help to the other.

The Chinese symbols of the heart, eyes and ears highlight a quality of listening that makes all the difference in changing our attitudes. It takes relationships to new levels of openness and honesty, of appreciation and gratitude, of intimacy and belonging. The ways in which we can often fail include judging the other as we listen, or dismissing silently what they say, or waiting impatiently for them to finish. We engage in this kind of listening at great cost to ourselves and to our relationships.

Listening is the pump that causes God's love, the 'Spring of living water', in us, to flow powerfully to our relationships, and to the world. Listening is a constant opportunity to deepen our vision as we journey into the mystery of God's love, the mystery of relationship and the mystery of life.

***Invitation:*** *When I really listen, the mystery of the other person unfolds.*

# Listen and Be Aware

- Listen and be aware of the freedom and power of the glorious vision of God.

- Listen and be aware that all things are possible with God. All things!

- Listen and be aware of the priceless gifts of wonder and gratitude, our travelling companions, always available to transform our lives.

- Listen and be aware of the delight of experiencing the gentle Christ, immediately present in oneself and in every person: 'Learn of me for I am gentle and humble in heart' *(Matthew 11:29).*

- Listen and be aware of the wonder of our being, one's own and that of every person, ennobled by the presence of the glorified Christ, making us models of love and peace to inspire others.

- Listen and be aware of the mystery of God's abundant life, unfolding within and before us, the peak experience of beauty and goodness without limit.

- Listen and be aware of God's abundant compassion and mercy in one's own life and in the lives of countless people.

- Listen and be aware of Christ with us, empowering us to love, rewarding us with the three joys of freedom, fruitfulness and fulfilment.

- Listen and be aware of the most precious gift of Christ's peace: 'My peace I leave you, my own peace I give you, a peace the world cannot give, that is my gift to you.'

- Listen and be aware of the dynamic presence of the Holy Spirit, everywhere at work, healing, integrating and transforming, drawing all people into God's Kingdom.

- Listen and be aware of the glory and bliss Christ has prepared for us in heaven: 'I go to prepare a place for you so that where I am you may be too' *(John 14:2,5).*

# Prayer as Listening

The most essential thing about prayer is that we listen to the Word,
Jesus, as he speaks to us in the Scriptures:
*'You do not ask for sacrifice and offering but an open ear' (Psalm 39:6).*

The practice of stillness, silence and listening
gives us a deep experience of the loving God:
*'Be still and know (experience) that I am God.' (Psalm 46:10).*

Listening needs to have reverence, (deep respect, love, wonder
and gratitude) if we are to be touched, healed,
informed and inspired by the word of God:
*Come and hear (listen) all you who revere God,*
*And I will tell you what he has done for me (Psalm 65:16).*

The prophet Isaiah makes an impassioned plea
that we listen to God, promising enormous benefits:
*'Listen, listen to me and you will have good things to eat*
*and rich food to enjoy. Pay attention; come to me,*
*listen and your soul will live' (Isaiah 55:2-3).*

The awareness of belonging to Jesus grows in us as we listen to him:
*'The sheep that belong to me listen to my voice' (John 10:27).*

Samuel's listening to God is a model for
the listening we need to bring to all prayer:
*'Speak, Lord, your servant is listening' (1 Samuel 3:10).*

When we listen with reverence and gratitude we create sacred space
for the transforming action of the Holy Spirit.
*'We do not know how to pray but the Spirit prays in us' (Romans 8:26).*

Isaiah encourages us to listen, remembering the life-long attentiveness
of the God who cares for us from the cradle to the grave.
*'Listen to me ... I have borne you from your birth,*
*carried you from the womb, even to your old age (Isaiah: 46:3-4).*

# Speaking With Love

It is often said that action speaks louder than words. This is true only when people do not mean what they say, or when they are not committed to the promises they make. Words are very powerful action when they are spoken with commitment, when for example, a committed couple declare their intention to love each other in marriage. We have many other examples of the power of committed speaking. We see the love Mother Teresa unleashed when she declared she was giving her life to ministering to the poorest of the poor. Nelson Mandela became a world figure because of his anti-apartheid leadership. It all began when he declared his commitment to this great cause.

We see the greatest action the world has ever known when God created the world by speaking it into existence. We read how God spoke everything into being: 'God said let there be light and there was light' *(Genesis 1:3)*. What an astonishing way to create! What an inspiring model God is for committed speaking, and what it can achieve. Since speaking consists of words and God is love, it follows that everyone and everything God created is a word of love spoken by God. Each of us is a priceless word of love spoken out of God's own mouth. We stand speechless in wonder, gratitude and reverence.

We see Christ in the Gospels using the power of speech to speak health into sick people, and life into those who were dead. When the leper asked to be cured, Christ responded simply, 'Be healed'. He restored the leper's health instantly through the use of words that were so simple, yet so astonishing. Even more astonishingly, we see him speaking life into Lazarus, dead for four days, with these spell-binding words: 'Lazarus, come forth.'

Christ continually brought comfort and strength to the broken and the wounded with words of gentleness and compassion. So we find in Christ a most gentle, compassionate and inspiring model of the miraculous power of words to heal and transform, and to raise self-esteem and confidence, when spoken with love and commitment.

We need a new awareness and respect for words, and their power, for they can heal or wound, build up or destroy. Wounds inflicted by angry, hurtful words may never heal. That is why we need to be aware of the way we speak, and how our words are affecting others. Life is a constant opportunity to be Christ-like in our speaking.

When we see with the compassionate eye, and listen with the sensitive ear, we will always speak the good word, the cheerful, welcoming word, the kind word, the gentle, healing word, the peaceful word, the caring, encouraging supportive word. Loving words heal, nourish and transform oneself, others, a relationship, a home, a workplace, a community, the human race.

***Invitation:*** *I am very aware of the extraordinary power of words.*

44

# The True Self Speaks

Studies have shown that the average person spends about ninety per cent of their waking hours in the negative world. We can only conclude that the false self is largely in control of most peoples' lives. We can have many fears, worries, anxieties, expectations, resentments and complaints. Worse still, we may bring little awareness to what we are doing to ourselves, and to those around us as we entertain regrets, resentments and worries. So we can easily be trapped in a world of misery and suffering.

If we step back and look at our lives, we may see that our lot is much better than we realise. We can start by bringing awareness to the abundant love in our hearts, deciding to let it flow to every person. Continuing to do this will transform our relationships. Even if some do not respond to our love and goodwill, we can still declare that our relationships are great. Jesus loved every one, but not everyone responded to him in love.

As our love flows we become more free, fruitful and fulfilled. This process, greatly enhanced by the practice of wonder and gratitude, benefits our mental, emotional, physical and spiritual health. Because of our overall wellness, we can declare that our health is great. We have outstanding models in those who turn serious ailments, pain and difficulty, into opportunity.

Having declared that both our relationships and our health are great, we can now declare that our life is great. Other reasons include the love and support we receive from so many, the countless gifts and opportunities we are given, the gift of ourselves to ourselves and to others, and the meaning, joy and fulfilment life gives us. The supreme gift is Jesus who cares for us and empowers us in a relationship of unconditional love.

We can now choose to make the following three declarations: my relationships are great, my health is great, my life is great. We need to make these declarations from the heart, with love and conviction, with passion and commitment. When declarations are made by the false self, doubt and uncertainty will always make success impossible. What will make the difference is remembering that Jesus is always with us, wanting to do infinitely more in us than we could ever ask or even imagine.

We allow him to act when we stand in true self awareness, making the above declarations. Attitudes of love will expand and deepen in a way that will surprise and transform us. We will enjoy an improved wellness on all levels, mental. emotional, physical and spiritual.

> **Invitation:**  *My relationships are great,*
> *My health is great,*
> *My life is great.*

# Loving Relationships

The deepest hunger of the human heart is undoubtedly the hunger for relationship. We long to connect and to bond with the loving God, with what is true and authentic in each person, and with the beauty and goodness that fill the universe. We are social beings, interdependent, in need of one another. We discover and realise ourselves only in relationship. We grow towards being fully alive and human in our relationship with God and with one another.

Loving relationships are fundamental to our lives. They heal us in our woundedness, and nourish us in our need to feel accepted and loved, appreciated and supported, encouraged and inspired. They give us an experience of belonging in a world of loneliness and alienation, and they set us free to be responsible, making love our great priority as we become fruitful and fulfilled.

How are we to establish and nourish loving relationships? Attitudes are the key. Loving attitudes bring great quality to our relationships, while selfish attitudes isolate us, damage our relationships, bringing suffering to self and to others. Relationship begins with the listening of the heart. This compassionate listening opens the heart, allowing the love in us to flow powerfully to each person we encounter. Most people will respond in love, causing loving relationships to take place. The open heart also speaks loving, encouraging words, affirming people and deepening relationships.

Loving relationships happen easily when we know who we are, when we understand ourselves and others as words of love spoken by God. Accepting that our core essence is love gives us an attitude of love, which is the power to create and nourish relationships.

This deeper understanding of the person is missing in much of today's culture, and has led to very superficial relationships. Lacking the deep respect for the sacred in self and in others, sex is merely casual or recreational, and relationships often end quickly. The person is only a thing, an experiment, and when one complains because the other is leaving, they are told to be free, grow up and move on. This reaction is a serious failure to be responsible, and a justification for use, abuse and betrayal.

The life of the Trinity, living in infinite love and harmony, is the model and foundation of all relationship. The infinite bliss of the divine relationships between the Father, the Son and the Holy Spirit, inspires and empowers us to keep on building loving relationships. The God of love is always with us, giving us an unlimited generosity to respond to the daily opportunities.

An intimate relationship with Jesus is available to everyone, and is easy to achieve. Living in our hearts, he is always inviting us into relationship. Relationship happens as we surrender to Jesus, allowing ourselves to be loved and supported by him. The love we experience brings an ease and a peace to our hearts and to our relationships.

The Beatitudes, because they are loving attitudes, are a wide open doorway to transform relationships. Each Beatitude is truly miraculous in its power to heal and transform relationships. The detachment and openness of the first Beatitude gives us the freedom to love with great generosity. We form great relationships when we respond to the invitation of the second Beatitude to be sensitive to the pain in others, and support them with our compassion.

The patience and unconditional acceptance of a gentle person guarantees excellent relationships. A gentle attitude dissolves fear, anger, insecurity, arrogance, etc., enabling a person to be themselves in the presence of a gentle person. That is why gentle people easily befriend those whom most people would find difficult. The practice of the Gentle Lifestyle keeps us constantly disposed to bring wonder, love and gratitude to all our relationships.

The hunger for justice of the fourth Beatitude gives us great respect for the sacredness of each person, which adds love and acceptance, strength and stability to our relationships. The mercy of the fifth Beatitude has unlimited power to forgive, to heal and to reconcile.

When we stand for the God-given goodness in people (sixth Beatitude), we bring much love and caring to our relationships. Our stand promotes an integrity and authenticity that communicates to others. People see that we are on their side, that our support is genuine. As relationships grow, communities of love are formed.

The peacemaker, like the gentle person, is a very attractive human being, before whom barriers of dislike and hostility, prejudice and ignorance disappear. The peacemaker is very successful because of their great respect for the person. They put their expectations aside, accepting and appreciating people as they are. The generosity and commitment of those who accept life with open arms, no matter the pain or tragedy it brings, transform relationships (eighth Beatitude). The practice of this Beatitude makes us powerful models of what love can do, especially the difference it makes to relationships.

By embracing the priceless gifts of wonder and gratitude, making them a frequent daily habit, we achieve a great freedom, love of life, and especially a love of people. Negative influences start to fade, and loving relationships become the heart and centre of life. Wonder and gratitude also open our eyes to the beauty and goodness of the world around us, to the gifts we use every day, and to the way our personal needs of body, mind, emotions and spirit are so well provided for.

Life is relationship, loving relationship, with self, others, God and creation. The invitation is to keep our minds and hearts open, allowing our love to flow. The rewards are enormous. We grow into an increasing freedom, we make an ever-growing difference in the lives of others, and we experience fulfillment.

***Invitation:*** *I take great delight in loving relationships.*

# The Great Choice

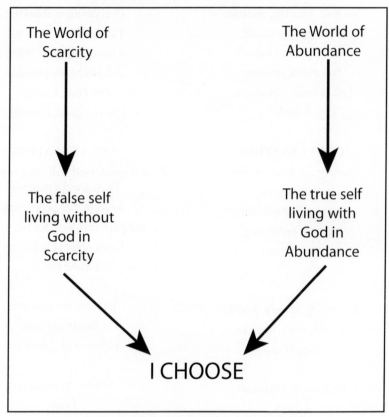

The World of
Scarcity

The World of
Abundance

The false self
living without
God in
Scarcity

The true self
living with
God in
Abundance

I CHOOSE

*In God's world the true self has unlimited space.*
*Everything in the world of abundance is music at its very best,*
*creating and expanding vision*
*and making life a dance or celebration of peak experience.*

The following three pages outline what these worlds consist of:

***Beliefs and Attitudes***

which lead to

***Conversation***

and the

***Results***

which follow.

| The World of Scarcity | The World of Abundance |
|---|---|
| **BELIEFS, ATTITUDES** | **BELIEFS, ATTITUDES** |
| No love, no trust, no time, | Everything is abundant |
| The world is unsafe, | The world is God's gift |
| I'm no good, I expect, | I have unlimited value |
| Not much possible | All things are possible |
| Life is hard, a problem, | with God. I accept. |
| I can't | Life is a great adventure |
| | |
| **CONVERSATION** | **CONVERSATION** |
| Scarcity: no time, no love, | God is good, God will always provide, |
| no energy, etc. | I can always manage. |
| Blaming, complaining, | I accept that people are |
| judging, criticising, | not perfect. I look for the good, |
| condemning. | I encourage, I build up, |
| | I make peace. |
| | |
| Regretting: if only, I wish, | I accept the past and |
| should, must, have to, | I live in the now, |
| ought to. | I choose to, I need to. |
| | |
| It's hard, it's difficult: | It's an opportunity: |
| I can't. | I can. |
| | |
| **RESULTS** | **RESULTS** |
| Expectations: fear, worry, | Life is a pilgrimage or |
| anxiety, unease, anger, | journey, an adventure full |
| frustration, violence in | of love, relationships, |
| thought, word, action: guilt, | caring, wonder, discovery, |
| shame, self-pity | risk, surprise, excitement, |
| dis-ease, misery. | passion, gratitude, |
| | fulfilment, delight, music! |
| | celebration, goodness. |

| The World of Scarcity | The World of Abundance |
| --- | --- |
| Boredom Responsibility a burden. | Every moment an opportunity to respond with abundance. |
| Stuck, a settler, security, comfort, attached to material things, status. | Free- spirited, a pilgrim, easily satisfied. |
| Indulging wants and desires, controlled by excesses and addictions. | Embracing moderation, giving power and freedom to be, to respond, to dance. |
| Low self-esteem causing insecurity, self-pity, dislike, prejudice, racism, controlling, manipulating. | Life is a mystery to be lived. Well-being of spirit, mind, emotions, body making us aware, alive, whole, complete, integrated. |
| The seven deadly sins: pride, greed, lust, anger, gluttony, envy, sloth. | The seven gifts of the Holy Spirit: wisdom, understanding, counsel, fortitude, knowledge, devotion to God and reverence for God. |
| Greed, power, oppression, injustice, abuse. Selfishness, competition, individualism. | Generosity, in relationship, cooperation, belonging. |
| Dealing with anger: violent, unforgiving, bitter, resentful, a victim. | Dealing constructively with anger: acknowledge, accept, communicate, forgive. See the opportunity. |

| The World of Scarcity | The World of Abundance |
|---|---|
| Pain and suffering: crippling. | Pain and suffering: accepting; Giving it meaning; an opportunity. |
| A sea of uncertainty and insecurity; a living hell in the black hole, the morass. | A thinking, reflective, contemplative attitude to life. Life is one continuing miracle of space, music, celebration and dance. |
| Hopelessness and despair. | The Good News of the Kingdom. |
| Denial of death or terror of death. | The hope of glory, heaven, death an intimate sister. |

## I Choose

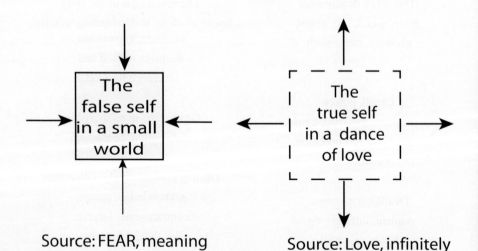

Source: FEAR, meaning
False Evidence Appearing Real

Source: Love, infinitely
abundant — God

# Choosing To Be Aware

## RESPONDING OR REACTING

### True Self Awareness
(The lens through which the true self sees life)
God is present, giving me an abundance of what I need.
Therefore I can respond in love, turning everything,
no matter how hard, into an opportunity.

### False Self Awareness
(The lens through which the false self sees life)
God is absent, what I need is always scarce. Therefore I react negatively,
seeing everything as hard, often so hard that I can't do countless things.

### Why is everything hard for the false self?
Because God is absent and all I have is scarcity.

### Why is everything an opportunity for the true self?
Because God is present giving me an abundance of patience,
kindness, generosity, etc., with which to respond.

### Conclusion:
At any given moment in our lives
what we see before us is either an opportunity or
something hard. We either respond with
love to the opportunity (true self) or we react with fear,
worry, blame, guilt, anger, aggression, impatience, etc., (false self).

### Invitation:
*Remember as often as possible to bring
the awareness of the true self to the moment.
Do it for the next twenty-one days,
the time it takes to form a habit.*

# My 8 Great Powers

*Read often with feeling, especially delight*

 God is always with me

 God gives me Abundance

 It's an Opportunity

 Yes, I can!

 I accept Responsibility

 I feel Wonder and Gratitude

 I Rest in Providence

 I stand for the Power of Love

# A New Awareness

When we see with the awareness of the true self, we marvel at the non-stop miracle of life, of God, the master craftsperson, at work in the universe. We are overwhelmed by the stunning order and precision regulating the planets and by the endless complexity, variety and beauty of creation. This is the awareness that sees the miracle of divine goodness, generosity and genius delighting in giving everything the stamp of uniqueness and originality. If we could only be aware, then life would be a continual joy and peak experience, and our hearts would overflow with love for God, life and every person. Everything would speak to us of God's loving and glorious presence.

How do we cultivate an awareness of this deeper dimension in life? Wonder is the great awakener, and we all have a great capacity for this gift, together with a hunger to use it. The practice of wonder uncovers the unlimited beauty, goodness and truth in nature and creation and especially in people. Delight and gratitude are an automatic response of the heart as the mystery of everyone and everything unfolds in peak experience.

The practice of wonder and gratitude give us a patient acceptance and joyful appreciation of life as it comes, and of people as they are. Adopting a listening, reflective attitude creates the space for surprise and wonder to occur spontaneously. We start to notice the hand of Providence at work beneath appearances.

The listening, reflective attitude, together with the practice of wonder and gratitude cultivate the contemplative lifestyle, for which we have a deep need. We go deeper by re-specting, seeing with the eyes of the true self, looking beyond surface appearances in creation, in events and especially in people. Beauty and goodness now take on an altogether new face.

We allow ourselves to be constantly surprised, astonished by the miracle of life, and the greatness in people. We respond with delight, with wonder and gratitude, to the God who gives us so much opportunity to live a full life.

At this deeper level everything is extraordinary. When we look with wonder at a flower we can see so much mystery, so much more than the scientists can explain. What we see is the gentle beauty of the face of God, manifested in the flower and in all creation.

St. Francis is a most inspiring model. For him every created thing was an intimate brother or sister, the beauty and goodness of which spoke to him of God's wondrous presence: brother sun, sister moon, brother fire, sister water. He must have responded with extraordinary love and gratitude, appreciation and delight. Awake, my soul, with a new and expanding awareness!

***Invitation:*** *I love to wonder and to ponder.*

# Experiencing the Presence

Could we stop to reflect on the stunning power of the divine Presence? The One who has created everything, the miracle universe too wonderful and mysterious to comprehend, is actually living his life in each of us: 'In him we live and move and have our being' *(Acts 17:20). The* power of Christ in us is an energy of pure love, cleansing, healing, nourishing, transforming, integrating, unifying. It is a power also that inspires us to move beyond our selfish interests to be one with Christ in his care and compassion for people.

What Jesus is doing is fulfilling his promise to draw all people, person by person, into the kingdom. 'When I am lifted up (on the cross and in the resurrection) I will draw all people to myself' *(John 12:32).* 'To myself' means to a relationship of the deepest love, intimacy and union. He invites us to cultivate this relationship: 'Make your home in me as I make mine in you.'

We do not even begin to appreciate the power of Jesus in our lives. We simply do not have the awareness. We can start to glimpse something of the reality, and grow steadily into a deeper awareness, if we use our sense of awe and wonder to feel amazed and astonished at the continuous miracle of life.

The miracle that everything exists when there might have been nothing. The miracle that the world is so full of love and generosity when there might have been no love whatever. And the most stunning miracle of all: that the loving God in the person of Jesus, who created this vast universe, actually lives his life in each of us, that he loves us totally and unconditionally, that he actually delights in us.

'Glory be to him, whose power working in us, can do infinitely more than we could ever ask or even imagine' *(Ephesians 3:20,21).* We need to feel this power of Christ's love in our hearts. We awaken it by feeling wonder and gratitude, amazement and astonishment. We deepen it with practice, and by feeling overwhelmed with reverence and delight at the miracle of it all.

Our experience will be deeper if we make the above passage personal: Glory be to you, Lord Jesus, your power working in us (us can include everyone and everything, as well as the affairs of the world, everything that glorifies Christ and is of value to the lives of human beings) is doing infinitely more than we could ever ask or even imagine.

***Invitation:*** *With gratitude I pray: 'Glory be to you, Lord Jesus.*
*Your power working in us is doing infinitely more*
*than we could ever ask, or even imagine.'*

# The Eight Beatitudes

### (Matthew 5:1-12)

The following are the Eight Beatitudes as contained in Matthew's Gospel. A brief explanation of each is given, followed by an invitation to adopt the new attitude by applying it to one's life.

1.  **'Blessed are the poor in spirit: theirs is the kingdom of heaven.'**

    Blessed those who are empty, detached and open for God and the abundance of his life. They experience a deep sense of belonging in God's kingdom of love and peace.

    *Invitation to the new attitude: Practice a healthy detachment, keeping everything in perspective. Keep God at the centre of life.*

2.  **'Blessed are those who mourn: they shall be comforted.'**

    Blessed are those who stand in the shoes of Jesus bringing his compassion to the pain and hurt, confusion and grief, they find in everyday people. Sensitive to the burdens they may be carrying, compassionate listening will provide a safe place to share what is troubling them.

    *Invitation to the new attitude: Listen with compassion and sensitivity to our own pain, the pain in each person we meet, and the pain of the world. Pray for the gift of tears, tears of sorrow for our sins, tears of compassion for the world, and tears of joy and gratitude at the healing power of the compassion of Jesus.*

3.  **'Blessed are the gentle: they shall have the earth for their heritage.'**

    Blessed are those who delight in the utter gentleness of the true self, made in God's own image and in whom the gentle Jesus lives. This gentle attitude allows him to satisfy their needs to the full.

    *Invitation to the new attitude: Experience the gentle Jesus through the daily practice of the Gentle Lifestyle.*

4.  **'Blessed are those who hunger and thirst for what is right: they shall be satisfied.'**

    Blessed are those who constantly grow in the awareness of the sacredness of the human person, the attitude that sees the soul in every person 'as big as an endless world, and like a blessed kingdom.' As this attitude grows they hunger for justice, doing what they can to create a more just world. The reward of this attitude is a profound peace and fulfilment.

    *Invitation to the new attitude: Be just in every relationship and be concerned for, and, if possible, active in local and international issues.*

5. **'Blessed are the merciful: they shall have mercy shown them.'**

Blessed are those whose eyes are open to the transforming power of mercy and forgiveness, healing the wounds of sin and division. Embracing this attitude, they give and receive God's mercy in abundance and superabundance.

*Invitation to the new attitude: Avail of every opportunity to deepen the attitude of mercy, forgiveness and reconciliation.*

6. **'Blessed are the pure in heart: they shall see God.'**

Blessed are those who are focused or single-minded, at one with Jesus in his love for the world. They will experience Jesus within.

*Invitation to the new attitude: Make a habit of taking stands (commitments), giving your life to something bigger than yourself, creating sacred space for Jesus to be miraculous.*

7. **'Blessed are the peacemakers: they shall be called sons and daughters of God.'**

Blessed are those who reject the conflict and disharmony that negative attitudes bring to life, choosing instead to be God's loving instruments in reconciling those who are in conflict, and deepening the peace of Christ in each person. They will enjoy the privilege of being daughters and sons of God.

*Invitation to the new attitude: Be aware of the presence of the Holy Spirit, making you a peacemaker in all your daily relationships.*

8. **'Blessed are those who are persecuted in the cause of right: theirs is the kingdom of heaven.'**

Blessed are those who, aware of Christ with them, make light of the suffering and difficulties of life, even to the point of persecution and death. Christ rewards them with the experience of belonging in God's kingdom.

*Invitation to the new attitude: Take advantage of the opportunity to respond with God's love to what is difficult or painful, turning everything into an opportunity.*

'My brothers, sisters, fill your minds with those things that are good and deserve praise: things that are true, noble, right, pure, lovely and honourable. And the God who gives us peace will be with you' *(Philippians 4:8-9).*

Loving attitudes are everything, the very heart and centre of life. They expand our hearts, allowing us to give and receive love more and more abundantly. And they give us the joy of the three Fs of love: freedom, fruitfulness and fulfilment.

***Invitation:** I embrace the eight Beatitudes wholeheartedly.*

# Beatitudes or Commandments?

When Jesus arrived on earth a total of six hundred and thirteen laws controlled peoples' lives. It was a society where expectations, what one should and should not do, dominated the life of each person. Jesus saw the tyranny of such a system, replacing it with a new and radical order. He invited people to sum up all these laws in the one law of love, outlined in the eight Beatitudes. The Beatitudes are a set of values or ideals, and they are also ways of giving and receiving love.

St. Paul, in his celebrated passage on love, concludes that even if we sell everything we own, and give it to the poor, it profits us nothing if we do not have love. So the motive is crucial. Doing the right thing because we think we should or because it is expected, profits us nothing, whereas the smallest act, undertaken with a motive of love, has unlimited value. Jesus spoke of the great value of the cup of water, given in his name.

Now that we have a higher and more empowering moral order, outlined in the Beatitudes, we ask if the commandments are of any value to us today? The commandments are fundamental but they are incomplete. It was to complete them that Jesus came, and he did so by putting them in a context of love, the meaning of which he spelled out in each of the Beatitudes.

When we compare the Commandments and the Beatitudes, we see that the former are much more limited and easier to keep. Rather than merely observing 'You must not kill', the Beatitudes invite us to feel compassion for the pain of the world, work for justice, extend mercy and give our lives to peacemaking.

We can feel we keep the commandments, yet live selfish lives: 'I'm a good Christian, I never do anyone any harm.' The purpose of life, however, is to make a difference, especially in the lives of the needy: 'I was hungry and you fed me, naked and you clothed me,' etc. Or: 'I was hungry and you never fed me, naked and you never clothed me,' etc. Through the practice of the Beatitudes we automatically keep the commandments but do much, much more.

To live the Beatitudes is to make a radical response to Christ's invitation to love. It is to step with passion and compassion into the shoes of the true self, becoming one with Christ in his love for the world. That is what it means to be a Christian, joyful, abundant and generous, taking advantage of the daily opportunities to put people first, especially those in most need.

Saints, the canonised and un-canonised, achieve greatness because they are inspired by the awareness of Christ always with them, and by what love can do. They live the Beatitudes with extraordinary love and generosity, patience and commitment, joy and celebration.

***Invitation:*** *I feel passion for what love can do.*

# The Gift of Being Empty

*'Blessed are the poor in spirit; theirs is the kingdom of heaven.'*
*(1st Beatitude)*

To be 'poor in spirit' is to know and accept in our hearts how utterly poor and needy we are. It is also to feel profound dependence on, and gratitude to, the God of infinite generosity who gives to us in such magnificent abundance. 'In spirit' means that we experience our need for God, and our gratitude to God, at the deepest level, in our spirit.

We have nothing that we can call our own. Everything is gift, and on loan, very temporary loan. Many live with the illusion that life goes on and on. That is why they get so attached and so possessive. Mother Teresa, bringing us face to face with reality, emphasised: 'I am nothing, I have nothing, I can do nothing (without God).' We are meant to use and enjoy God's gifts. It is the attachment, the possessiveness and the greed of the false self that destroy our lives.

In India monkeys are captured by putting sweet meat in a glass container with a narrow opening. The container is then buried in the ground with the opening at ground level. When a monkey grabs hold of the sweetmeat it cannot now remove its paw because the opening is too narrow. The monkey sacrifices its freedom and its life because it will not let go.

What makes monkeys of us? What keeps us so attached? It is first of all a failure to reflect – 'the unexamined life is not worth living.' We can easily drift into the 'security' of comfortable, selfish attitudes and behaviour, the 'far country' of the prodigal son.

The choice is to stay attached like the monkey, or to let go and be free like the prodigal son who returned home to the father's love. We need to choose to be open to God's love, and the love of others, aware that the two-way street of love is what gives meaning and fulfilment. Nothing else!

Being busy, running away from ourselves, is one of the most damaging and widespread attachments of today's world. Worry is also very destructive as people often turn vice into virtue: 'who will do the worrying if I don't?' Others confuse worry with responsibility: 'of course I worry about my children, I'm a responsible parent.' Many get trapped in their attachment to money and possessions. Others get attached to hurts, pain and insecurities, and can use them to get attention.

Other common attachments include regretting, blaming, complaining, criticising, judging, and having expectations of self, others, life and God. We can be attached to many other things including alcohol, drugs, security, sex, power, control, sport, talking, gossiping, prejudice, intolerance, family, friends, laziness. The list goes on: selfishness, pride, arrogance, contempt, envy, anger, aggression, impatience, resentment, lying, stealing, insincerity, hypocrisy, illness, denial, etc.

We can be very attached, or even addicted, to some of the items on the above list. How can we stay so attached, refusing to let go until our lives are taken from us? The crucial thing is to recognise that we have a choice, and then be honest, admitting to ourselves what these attachments are. Then we need to let go of our attachments and get our lives back.

We could spare ourselves much suffering if only we would be honest and detach. Mother Teresa used to compare life to a cup: 'If the cup is full (of attachments) how can God put anything in it?' Until we detach we prevent God from giving us the necessities of life: freedom, love, wisdom, inner peace, etc.

## JESUS AND ST. FRANCIS

Detachment and emptiness open up an ever expanding world of possibility, a world of love and generosity, of adventure and discovery, of beauty, wonder and peak experience. Other ingredients central to this world include celebration, joy and gratitude, fulfilment and peace. This is the abundance Jesus offers to those who are willing to detach and be free.

The emptiness or poverty of Jesus was a most astonishing mystery. He was both God and man, but chose to be empty of divine power. He preferred to be seen as an ordinary Jew. He hid behind his miracles, warning those he cured to tell no one. He allowed himself to be vulnerable, to be arrested, scourged, mocked and crucified.

'Though he was in the form of God, Jesus did not count equality with God a thing to be grasped. He emptied himself taking the form of a servant *(Philippians 2:6-7).*' Having demonstrated its deepest meaning, Jesus has become our supreme model of emptiness or detachment,

St, Francis had a most profound appreciation of the value of emptiness or poverty. After his conversion he told his friends of his passion for the new love of his life. They waited expectantly to meet the new woman who turned out to be Lady Poverty. Francis practiced such detachment and poverty that his heart was wide open with sacred space for God and God's abundant love. He thus achieved a love and a joy unparalleled in history. More than eight hundred years on, he is still a most inspiring model, worldwide.

Before the process of becoming detached, empty and open can begin, we need to accept that we have a need to change and then be willing to change. To change is to re-pent, to re-think, and this needs to be a daily and life–long process. 'To live is to change, to be perfect is to have changed often.' In our weak and wounded condition we need strength from on high. That is why a heart-to-heart relationship with Jesus is so essential. As we experience his unconditional love, we grow into a deep freedom and detachment.

***Invitation:*** *I model myself on Jesus, our loving servant.*

# Acceptance

We generate the detachment of the first Beatitude when we make up our minds to practise acceptance. Acceptance includes the acceptance of the loving God, of self and others as we all are, and of life as it comes. We accept that God loves us unconditionally. We accept human weakness in ourselves and in others, and especially the truth of who we are: priceless words of love spoken by God.

We take a major step towards acceptance when we put a stop to blaming, complaining, criticising, judging and making assumptions; when we let go of having to be right; when we put aside our expectations of self, others, life and God; when we forgive, letting go of resentment and bitterness; when we stop trying to control others and life.

Instead, we accept, without evaluating or judging, allowing the abundant love in us to flow to everyone. Acceptance also puts aside regrets: what is is, what has happened has happened. And we trust that Jesus, in his infinite compassion, brings good out of everything: mistakes, injustices, horrors, tragedies, no matter how great the scale.

The gift of acceptance is great because of the freedom it brings to both mind and heart. Acceptance also strengthens the will, enabling us to be love, to be who we are as God created us. And to choose love, learning to do what love needs us to do, and inspires us to do. We then arrive at a place of inner peace. And so the practice of acceptance generates the three Fs of love: freedom, fruitfulness and fulfilment.

Knowing in one's heart that 'I can' is at the root of acceptance. I can accept because the God of love is always with me, giving me an abundance of what I need to accept self, each person and life as it unfolds. The alcoholic's prayer, used often, is a powerful generator of acceptance.

'God grant me the serenity to accept the things I cannot change, courage to change the things I can, and wisdom to know the difference.' What we need is the wisdom to see what can and cannot be changed, and the courage to act when the situation is so urgent that it cannot be postponed.

The constant practice of our travelling companions, wonder and gratitude, or any of the tools we have been discovering, will give us the inner peace and strength to establish and deepen the attitude of acceptance. We have great models to inspire us. Jesus, accepting his death without a murmur, is our supreme model. A young mother said: 'I'm dying of cancer and have a short time to live. I'm not sad because I'm going to God. I have three young children and a wonderful husband, and I know my children will be very well looked after.'

***Invitation:*** *I can accept because Jesus is always with me.*

61

# Struggle: A Necessity

A man found a cocoon of the emperor moth and took it home. He watched it as it emerged. One day a small opening appeared, and for several hours the moth struggled, but seemed unable to force its body past a certain point.

Deciding something was wrong, the man took a scissors and snipped the remaining bit of cocoon. The moth emerged easily, its body large and swollen, the wings small and shrivelled.

The man expected that in a few hours the wings would spread out in their natural beauty, but nothing happened. Instead of developing into a creature free to fly, the moth spent its life dragging around a swollen body and shrivelled wings.

The constricting cocoon and the struggle necessary to pass through the tiny opening are God's way of forcing fluid from the body into the wings. The 'merciful' snip was, in reality, cruel. – *(From 'Quote' Magazine.)*

Life is both a test and a choice. We are constantly presented with opportunities to move from the resistance of the false self to the freedom of the true self. When we find the struggle difficult we can easily get discouraged, allowing the false self to take control. We can struggle with personal weaknesses, with depression in ourselves or a family member or with other health problems. Or the struggle could be with tensions in marriage or family life, or with difficulties at work, or we could have difficulties with neighbours. We make the struggle more stressful when we resist, try to control, fail to accept or do our best to find a peaceful solution.

We need to ask who or what we are attached to and do not want to let go of? Who or what we are unwilling to accept? Who or what causes us to be discouraged or angry, to blame or complain. The opportunity is to let go of our resistance, our unwillingness to detach, and then to accept, creating sacred space for God to give us what we need.

Working through our struggles is exactly what we need if we are to overcome the resistance of the false self, becoming empty and detached, humble and gentle, patient and generous. Open to Christ and to others, we accept graciously the love and support that people offer us. There may be times when we need to be humble enough to request support.

As we work through our struggles we learn to accept self and others as we all are, and life as it comes with all its joys and peak experiences, all its pain and difficulties; all its injustice, oppression and selfishness. Surrendering to Providence, we see the opportunity in everything to grow patiently towards becoming whole and integrated, the unique, loving, self-expressed, human beings, God intends us to be.

**Invitation:** *I accept the opportunity my struggles offer me.*

# Mother Teresa's Letter

You have said 'yes' to Jesus and he has taken you at your word. And so this terrible emptiness that you experience. God cannot fill what is full. He can fill only emptiness, deep poverty, and your 'yes' is the beginning of being or becoming empty.

It's not how much we really 'have' to give, but how empty we are, so that we can receive fully in our life and let Jesus live his life in us. In you today, he wants to relive his complete submission to his Father. Allow him to do so. Take away your eyes from yourself and rejoice that you have nothing, that you are nothing, that you can do nothing (without God).

Give Jesus a big smile, each time your nothingness frightens you. This is the poverty of Jesus. You and I need to let him live in us and through us in the world.

Keep giving Jesus to your people not by words, but by your example, by your being in love with Jesus, by radiating his holiness and spreading his fragrance of love everywhere you go.

Just keep the joy of Jesus as your strength. Accept whatever he gives, and give whatever he takes with a smile. You belong to him. Tell him: I am yours, and if you cut me to pieces every single piece will be yours. Let Jesus be the victim and the Priest in you.

*(This letter was a reply to a priest who complained about being empty).*

## A CONCLUSION

Because love is who we are, it is our nature to love each person. If we are slow to give generously of ourselves, then we do both ourselves and the world a serious injustice. When we withhold our love we suffer by cutting ourselves off from the flow of love that is coming to us from so many. Those we interact with also suffer by being deprived of our love and support.

Every person deserves to be loved and respected, because of who they are, each a word of love spoken by God. That is why Jesus told us to love even our enemies. Some believe that they have a right to remain angry with those who do wrong. We can only heal ourselves and the world through our compassion for the abuser and the abused, for the oppressor and the oppressed.

The practice of generosity always creates a win-win situation, while our failure to deal with what closes the heart, fear, worry, anger, unforgiveness, selfishness, inhibitions, etc., makes everyone a loser. We are all deprived of the great joys of love that nourish and transform our lives. These joys include freedom which brings out the best in us, and fruitfulness, as our hearts open and our love flows to heal and nourish the world, giving us a fulfilment that lights up our lives.

*Invitation: With an open heart I allow Jesus to be my strength.*

# The Joy of Compassion

*'Blessed are those who mourn: they shall be comforted.'*

*(2nd Beatitude)*

The life of Jesus was one of extraordinary compassion. We see it in the Gospel story as he interacted with those in pain and grief. When he was mourning over Jerusalem he was extending compassion to all people of all time in their pain and suffering. On the cross his compassion flowed abundantly to the pain and grief of every person. It is natural, therefore, that Jesus would make compassion a Beatitude, inviting us to be one with him in his compassion for all people in their pain, grief and struggle.

The suffering of the world is immense, far beyond anything we can imagine. Job, inconsolable in his grief, pleaded aloud for compassion. Most of the world's pain pleads in silence. Job is God's mouthpiece, pleading with us now to bring the compassion of Jesus to the pain of the world.

This Beatitude comes alive when we bring a sensitive, compassionate attitude to all our relationships, and when we include the plight of the oppressed in our thoughts and prayers. We need to expand our awareness to include the victims of poverty and injustice, tragedy and disaster, worldwide. We can easily cut ourselves off from the burden of pain and grief that others carry. Safe and unaware inside our comfort zones, we can settle for a life of mediocrity.

The invitation is to be aware of the privilege of standing in the shoes of Jesus, feeling inspired and empowered to be in action with this Beatitude as we interact daily with people. The invitation is also to appreciate ourselves as an endless spring of the living water of divine compassion, and as a constantly expanding possibility for the healing power of compassion.

We bring wonder and gratitude to the miracle of not only being the instruments of Jesus and his compassion, but also of receiving so much support in our own neediness. Our hearts are enriched with a deepening experience of the three Fs of love, the joys of freedom, fruitfulness and fulfilment. These joys are the blessedness Jesus promises to those who give themselves wholeheartedly to the ministry of compassion.

Sometimes we may feel unable to care for others in their pain because of our own burden of pain and grief. There are times when we all need to hear the gentle invitation of Jesus and feel his healing touch: 'Come to me all you who labour and are overburdened, and I shall give you rest' *(Matthew 11:29)*. This is the encounter that inspires us to be one with Jesus in embracing the pain of the world with his compassion. Supporting people with the compassion of Jesus is the essence of this Beatitude.

***Invitation:*** *I feel compassion for the pain in each person.*

64

# The Gift of Tears

How we fail to recognise the gifts of God! And how diminished we become as a result. Tears are one such gift. Inhibited by feelings of shame and guilt, we may fail to shed tears when it would be of great benefit to oneself and to others to do so. Tears, helping us to empathise with people in their grief, are an important part of this Beatitude of mourning.

Tears have many benefits. They heal us in time of loss and grief. They deepen sorrow for our sins, and generate mercy for the sins of the world. They expand our heart with compassion for the pain of every person. And they fill us with joy and gratitude at the healing power of Christ's compassion. These benefits are of such enormous value that we can ill-afford to prevent our tears from flowing when a situation requires it.

Jeremiah, the prophet, deeply troubled by the plight of the Jewish people, asked God for an abundance of tears: 'Let my eyes run down with tears night and day.' Christ was very comfortable with tears. He wept when his friend Lazarus died, when he foresaw the destruction of Jerusalem and in his agony in the garden. 'During his life on earth Christ offered up prayer and entreaty, aloud and in silent tears' *(Hebrews 5:7).*

The Desert Fathers put great emphasis on the gift of tears, encouraging people to pray constantly for this gift. Until we receive it, they said, our love and compassion could not expand and deepen. It is not necessary that tears always flow. We can cry in our hearts in the sense that we empathise, feeling how it is for those who are oppressed by the burden of loss, grief, loneliness, injustice, poverty, etc.

Christ weeps daily through the eyes of the oppressed, in homes, workplaces, prisons, hospitals, etc., as the strong oppress the weak, and as people struggle to cope with their pain. Can we be one with Christ in feeling the pain of the world, in supporting the weak, the vulnerable and the helpless? Can we be one with him in deep, heart-felt prayer, in allowing our tears to flow, and in the way we empathise with those in grief and pain?

We can allow our compassion to flow to these, our little brothers and sisters, in our thoughts and prayers, and sometimes in our tears, and by holding them in our sacred space in the Abundance Prayer.

The gift of tears also enables us to give profound meaning to our own pain, suffering and struggle. We can offer it, in union with Christ's suffering, for the alleviation of the world's suffering, and for the freedom of all persons to live in peace, able to take responsibility for their own lives, rather than being controlled by others.

***Invitation:*** *I pray daily for the gift of tears.*

# The Meaning of Gentleness

*'Blessed are the gentle: they shall have the earth for their heritage'*

*(3rd Beatitude)*

In the secular world gentleness is dismissed. It is seen as weakness, lacking the confidence and backbone that compel respect, and the cutting edge necessary to make it in life. True gentleness could not be more different.

We see the meaning of gentleness in the person of Jesus or a Mother Teresa and we are filled with reverence. We feel inspired. Jesus was gentle towards everyone, even the Pharisees who wanted to kill him. Even when he knew Judas was about to betray him, Jesus showed him the most remarkable gentleness. Jesus saw gentleness as so fundamental that he invited us to model our life on the gentleness we see in him: 'Learn of me for I am gentle and humble in heart.' In this Beatitude he promises that the gentle attitude allows all our needs to be answered.

To be gentle is to be empty, open and free, free to be oneself and allow each person to be free. To be gentle is to listen with sensitivity and patience, and to speak healing, encouraging words. To be gentle is to be caring, making people feel special, wanted, loved and supported. To be gentle is to be aware of the gentle Jesus in oneself and in each person. Drawing on the gentleness of Jesus, we feel empowered to be gentle like him and with him.

Recognising that all is gift, the gentle person is deeply humble and grateful. The gentle have a special gift for hospitality, welcoming every person with generosity. That means that he or she is continually creating communities of love, where each person feels they belong. The gentle person is big enough to embrace all the world, and compassionate enough to embrace each person.

Gentleness has great strength and is resilient in the face of injustice, pain and difficulty. Jesus was fearless in condemning injustice. Gentleness has the courage and strength to accept responsibility, overcoming the weakness that wants to opt out, or blame, complain or judge, or lapse into worry and anxiety, allowing fear to take over.

The practice of gentleness gives us extraordinary benefits. It opens the heart to patient acceptance and joyful appreciation of life as it comes, and to people as they are. Bringing much cheerfulness and wonder to life, gentleness creates frequent peak experiences for self and others.

The radical and empowering vision of gentleness given by this Beatitude, gives us a heart rich in love and generosity. That is why the gentle person has it all. Living in the now of true self awareness, he or she brings deep appreciation and gratitude to God's countless gifts and blessings.

***Invitation:*** *Jesus, give me a gentle heart.*

# A Profile of the Gentle Self

- In my gentle self I am listening attentively, aware, fully present. Responding to the opportunity of the moment with grace and gratitude. In my gentle self I am grateful, prayerful.

- In my gentle self I am tender, vulnerable, humble. Strong, resilient, courageous, decisive, confident. Wise, intuitive, sensitive. Balanced, flexible, spontaneous, free of expectations, able to be and let others be. I am each of these things when the occasion requires it.

- In my gentle self I am silent, peaceful, patient, non-violent. Pure, single-minded. Trusting, surrendering. Open, able to request. This is who I am in my true self, the self that God has created in God's own image.

- In my gentle self I am abundant. Generous in giving of self, time and resources. Courteous, respectful. In relationship with Christ and the true self in every person. What a miracle!

- In my gentle self I am compassionate, merciful, forgiving. Non-judgmental, non-threatening, supportive. Warm, intimate, belonging. Delighting to put people before selfish interests. In my gentle self, my true self, I have all these gifts in abundance, God-given.

- In my gentle self I am honest, loyal, truthful. In harmony with conscience. Decisions and behaviour are always appropriate. I am my own person. How generous Christ is to me!

- In my gentle self I have great capacity for surprise, awe, wonder, astonishment and mystery. Living the adventure of life to the full. Delighting in God's beauty and goodness. Dancing with the universe. This is the reality of my gentle self. How astonishing!

- In my gentle self I have a vision that is unlimited, filling me with passion and aliveness. In my gentle self I'm unshakable and unstoppable (when I surrender to the truth of all the above qualities). Christ has endowed me with all these sublime gifts.

- I thank you, Lord for the wonder of my being and that of every person, and the miracle of your presence in me and in every person.

*(This profile, created from the pages of the Gospel, is a profile of both the gentle Christ and the true self in each person).*

# Experiencing the Essence

In his celebrated passage on love, St. Paul spells out beautifully the meaning of love as well as its application to all our attitudes and behaviour. To emphasise that love is, in its essence, gentle, we could add the words 'gentle love', each time the word love is used in the passage.

Love, gentle love, is always patient and kind; love, gentle love, is never jealous; love, gentle love, is never boastful or conceited; love, gentle love, is never rude or selfish; love, gentle love, does not take offence. Love, gentle love is not resentful.

Love, gentle love, takes no pleasure in other people's sins but delights in the truth. Love, gentle love, is always ready to excuse, to trust, to hope. Love, gentle love, is always ready to endure whatever comes. Love, gentle love, does not come to an end. There are three things that last: faith, hope and love, gentle love; and the greatest of these is love, gentle love *(See 1 Corinthians 13:4–13)*.

The meaning of this passage is clear and easily understood. What we need, however, is to be able to experience the healing, nourishing power of gentleness, and also be inspired to practice it with great freedom and generosity. We need it, our relationships need it and the world needs us to be models of this gentle love.

The key to this inner experience is to go through the passage spending time on each line. We ponder its priceless beauty, feeling delight and gratitude. We feel as deeply as possible the energy of God's gentle love expanding our hearts, filling our whole being, and flowing out to the world. We feel it, we savour it and we experience it.

We surrender to it, allowing it to take hold of us, mind and heart, body and soul. We internalise it, allowing it to be who we are. We feel delight and gratitude as we allow our whole person to be immersed in this miracle of gentle love, making us one with the gentle Christ and with the gentle self, in each person.

As we experience gentleness we connect with the sacred in ourselves and in others, feeling deep reverence. 'The spring of living water', God's gentle love in us, flows powerfully to everyone. Generosity takes hold of us, and we become a constantly expanding power of gentle love and support in the lives of others.

*Invitation: I feel delight at the precious gift of Christ's gentle love.*

# The Gentle Lifestyle

1. Gentleness is thinking gentle thoughts about self, others, life and God.

2. Gentleness is feeling God's energy of gentle love filling one's whole being and flowing out to the world. (We are fields of gentle energy).

3. Gentleness is listening attentively to each person with God's energy of gentle love.

4. Gentleness is speaking gently so that what we say will build up and do good to others.

5. Gentleness is doing the loving thing as we work for a better and more just world.

6. Gentleness is making sacrifices (offerings made sacred by the motive of love) not only because love requires them, but also because love inspires us to make them.

7. Gentleness is the awareness and discipline to look after our health and well-being responsibly.

8. Gentleness is turning every difficulty and adversity into an opportunity.

9. Gentleness is feeling wonder and gratitude before the mystery of God, life and creation.

10. Gentleness is resting in the comfort of Providence, empowering our stands, our lives and the affairs of the world.

*Invitation: I am inspired by the power of the Gentle Lifestyle.*

# The Meaning of Justice

*'Blessed are they who hunger and thirst for justice'*
*(4th Beatitude)*

To understand the meaning of justice, we need to see it from a divine rather than a human perspective. The justice of God needs to be seen in the light of the infinite mercy and compassion of God. To be just, we need to submit to God, to God's law, and to the way God chooses to do things. We also need to have our hearts transformed by the compassion and mercy of God.

Justice accepts the truth that we are all equal, each a word of love spoken by God. Christ sacrificed himself to teach us respect for the dignity and sacredness of the person, and to unite the human race as one family in a full sharing of the glory and bliss of heaven.

Justice sees clearly that we are pilgrims and strangers on this earth. We can call nothing our own. Everything is on temporary loan, even our bodies. This awareness does much to free us from being selfish, over-possessive and attached to the things of this life. Aware that we are all brothers and sisters, God's children, we appreciate the need to do our best for others, sharing our time and resources, especially with those in greatest need.

Justice means right relationship with every person and with creation. We achieve this quality as we educate our conscience, becoming aware of our responsibilities. The Bible emphasises compassion towards all those oppressed by injustice, those who are most helpless, and those in greatest need. A social conscience, giving us a strong sense of justice, is one of the great cornerstones of life.

Aware of the eternal value of every person, justice means having deep respect for each one, being a good neighbour, and caring for people in whatever way we can. Justice asks what we can do for travelling people, immigrants, asylum seekers, solo parents, those with addictions, the sick, prisoners, the old, the lonely, victims of bullying, etc. Justice is honest with self and others, and honest in business. Justice means paying our debts and our taxes.

We will judge ourselves according to the quality of justice we have practiced in our lifetime: 'I was hungry and you fed me, I was lonely and you visited me. I was sick or in prison and you came to see me, etc.' Or: 'I was hungry and you never fed me, lonely and you never visited me, sick or in prison and you never came to see me, etc.'

We grow in the hunger and thirst for justice as we feel the wonder of who each person is: a unique, priceless and exquisite word of love spoken by God. This understanding of the human person gives us a deep compassion, and an appreciation of the urgency of justice.

*Invitation: I grow daily in my hunger for justice.*

# Inspired and Empowered

A story is told about Michelangelo, who was working on a large block of marble. A passer-by stopped to watch. Not knowing Michelangelo or anything about sculpture, he asked what he was doing. Michelangelo, full of excitement, responded: 'there's an exquisite angel locked up inside this block of marble and I can't wait to let it out of its prison.' He then resumed his work with great passion. He is said to have had the energy of three men. This energy flowed from his vision. He saw an angel where most people would see only a piece of marble.

Who am I in the story? I am the block of marble, consisting of the exquisite angel and the waste marble. The angel is the true self, the one endowed with the gift of vision. I am also the waste marble that imprisons me, what creates and feeds the false self. This waste includes the false beliefs we accept as true, 'I'm not good enough', everything is scarce, life is hard, etc. The waste marble also includes blaming, complaining, criticising, judging, regretting, etc., as well as fear, worry, anxiety, pride, arrogance, greed, injustice, having expectations and wanting to control, etc. These negative influences disempower the Michelangelo, the true self, in each of us. That is why, whenever we notice them, we need to take appropriate action to set ourselves free.

I am Michelangelo in the story, inspired with the vision that sees angels, the exquisite beauty of the true self in every person but especially in those oppressed by injustice. I am Michelangelo, the passionate sculptor, empowered by the awareness that God is with me, giving me a hunger and thirst for justice, and making me fearless and unstoppable in working for justice. Michelangelo said sculpture was easy. 'All I'm doing is removing the waste marble from what is already there.'

It is our life's work to remove the 'waste marble' from our lives, to change the negative beliefs, attitudes and conversation that disempower us. Our task is also to remove the 'waste marble' of injustice that plagues the world. I can sometimes be the bystander in the story, indifferent, sitting on the fence, observing life, settling for safety and mediocrity, never committing to anything, failing to be just.

This great story inspires us to be passionate in our hunger and thirst for justice, taking responsibility, doing all in our power to improve peoples' lives by making the world a more just place. The awareness of the true self tells us that we are all Michelangelos. Christ is with us, giving us what we need to turn every injustice into an opportunity to work for justice. We always have what it takes, and more. That is why we can choose to be inspired. All things are indeed possible with God.

***Invitation:*** *I am a Michelangelo for justice.*

# We are Royalty

A story is told of invaders who came and conquered the country. They killed the king, the queen and their children. A servant rescued their baby girl and gave her to a poor family. She grew up believing herself to be the daughter of her adopted family. One day she met an old lady who asked: 'do you know who you are?' 'Yes,' she said, 'I am the daughter of the potato pickers.' 'No, you're not, you're the daughter of the royal family who were murdered by the invaders,' said the old lady.

From that moment on everything changed for the young woman because now she knew who she was, royalty. She continued to pick potatoes but now she did it differently. The surge in confidence and self-esteem she experienced gave her life an altogether new meaning, and purpose. Now she had a smile on her face and a spring in her step. She had simply come alive. For the first time in her life someone told her who she was, and her hungry heart was overwhelmed by the good news, which set her free to be fruitful and fulfilled.

Who am I in the story? I am the young woman, perhaps badly in need of someone, anyone, who will tell me who I am, giving my self-esteem and confidence a much needed boost. Life constantly presents us with opportunities to show interest in others, as people cry out, mostly in silence, for love and support. The listening ear and the loving word have great power.

Scripture inspires us by telling us that we are royalty, princes and princesses in God's household: 'You are a chosen race, a royal priesthood, a consecrated nation, a people set apart' *(1 Peter 2:9)*. The conclusion is that each of us is enormously privileged. Awareness of who we really are, gives us numerous benefits, especially a strong sense of justice, and an urgency to do what we can.

In the story I am also the old lady, the wisdom figure who sees beyond the brokenness, the woundedness and the oppression that obscure or hide the true self in others. Aware of the riches of love and wisdom Jesus gives us, we can see what is great in people, and reveal it to them. We know we can make a difference by listening with a compassionate heart, and by speaking words of love and encouragement, as we build their self-esteem and confidence.

A hunger and thirst for justice, just love, will be a major value in our lives when we realise how privileged we are. An attitude of deep respect will be present in our relationships making us more just and more caring. When the occasion arises we will want to enrol others in a cooperative effort to deal with issues of injustice. We will be rewarded with the great joys of love: freedom, fruitfulness and fulfilment.

***Invitation:*** *If we only knew the power of God!*

# The Freedom of Mercy

*'Blessed are the merciful: they shall obtain mercy.'*
*(5th Beatitude)*

The scale of the world's injustice, oppression and inhumanity is far too great to even imagine. The atrocities of the last century are nothing new in history. We all contribute to the global pain and dysfunction, for we all sin and carry a burden of guilt: 'All have sinned and fall short of the glory of God.'

In the face of so great an accumulation of sin and suffering, perpetrated by every member of the human race, we need a God of unbounded mercy. Jesus is that miracle God. From the cross he forgave us all, no matter how great our crimes. He saw the true self, his own image, in every person. With this focus he was able to offer the greatest prayer ever known, embracing all people of all time: 'Father, forgive them, they know not what they do.'

We can turn to Jesus at any time, certain to experience his mercy and peace. That may not satisfy us fully because we all have a deep need to speak the things that trouble us. That is why a person will sometimes take advantage of a chance encounter to open their heart to a sympathetic stranger. People go to A.A. meetings, not only for support, but also to confess what troubles their conscience. These encounters are sacred moments where the person meets the merciful Jesus in the other person, or in the members of the group.

In the Catholic tradition we have a sacrament of mercy, what is called the sacrament of reconciliation and peace. Encountering the merciful Jesus in this sacred ritual, we are forgiven for our wrongdoing, and reconciled with the Father and the community. Reconciliation is necessary because all sin, no matter how private we think it is, has a social effect: we are fields of energy, and sin causes us to communicate negative energy to the world. The sacrament can be a peak experience if we stand in the shoes of the prodigal son, picturing Jesus standing in front of us, full of delight, his arms outstretched to embrace us. He will transform our hearts with a new surge of mercy and forgiveness towards the world, giving us a deep experience of the three Fs of love: freedom, fruitfulness and fulfilment.

The challenge is to keep growing into a deeper attitude of mercy. We can give ourselves a great boost by seeing ourselves as a constantly expanding possibility for more and more mercy. The idea of an expanding heart changes our perspective profoundly. Instead of being stuck in how hard it is to forgive, we come to see that we always have abundant mercy. We move from 'it's hard' to 'it's an opportunity'. An enthusiastic awareness of who we are – 'I am a constantly expanding possibility for mercy and forgiveness' – will move us effortlessly to this new place of empowerment.

***Invitation:*** *Lord, make me an instrument of your mercy.*

# Freedom to Forgive

People sometimes have great difficulty in forgiving, and can become discouraged by their continual failure. No matter how great our difficulty in forgiving, or how deep-seated our anger or resentment, we can take steps to achieve freedom.

Hidden feelings are often the underlying cause of the difficulty. One solution consists in finding a good listener, someone we can trust. We can then explore our feelings of injustice and hurt, anger and resentment, bringing them to the surface, making them conscious. A safe atmosphere is essential. We need to talk about our feelings and our fear of looking at them. We need to keep talking and feeling as we try to make the feelings conscious. It is very helpful to name the feelings. The following sacred ritual is extremely effective for those who have difficulty in forgiving:

- Find a quiet place where you will not be disturbed.

- Light a candle and spend a little while letting it speak to you of the presence of Jesus, the Light, helping you with his gentle, merciful love.

- Then write spontaneously, allowing your feelings to surface. Write whatever comes to mind. Do not reflect as you write, or read over what you have written. The purpose of the exercise is to set yourself free from this toxic energy, not reinforce it. Stay in touch with what you are feeling.

- When you have written all you can, burn the page(s) from the flame of the candle. Let the ash fall into the wash hand basin with a white surface. Be aware of the flame of the candle representing the flame of God's love, burning away the poison of anger and bitterness, as well as healing your pain and hurt, and building your confidence and self-esteem.

- When the burning is complete, turn on the tap and observe the water removing all the ash. Let the water remind you of the ongoing power of the water of baptism, cleansing you of the venom of bitterness and resentment that you have got in touch with.

- Be aware of the freedom of God's mercy and forgiveness, empowering you to be your true self, able to be merciful towards all. 'Glory be to you, Lord Jesus, your power working in us is doing infinitely more than we could ever ask or even imagine.'

- When all the ash has disappeared, observe the white, clean surface of the basin. Let it remind you of how clean and pure you have become. Repeat this ritual daily until there is nothing more you can write. Do the exercise whenever old hurts resurface or new ones occur. Conclude with a silent prayer of deep reverence and gratitude.

***Invitation:*** *Jesus helps me as I help myself.*

# Freedom Achieved

Seven is a sacred number in the Bible, and we can use this number to our great advantage. The following exercise is based on Christ's response to Peter when he asked if he should forgive seven times. 'Not only seven, but seventy times seven.' The exercise consists of writing the following line seventy times a day for seven days, allowing God's mercy to flow freely to anyone we are afraid of or anyone we have difficulty in accepting or forgiving:

*With you, Jesus, I declare their innocence.*

As we write we can picture and be aware of Christ standing beside the person(s) with whom we are concerned. We write with enthusiasm and gratitude, aware that the gift of tender mercy is transforming the fear or anger or resentment in oneself as well as the darkness in those we are praying for. If we suffer from guilt or low self-esteem we can use the following line:

*With you, Jesus, I declare my innocence.*

- We can use this exercise to reconcile those in conflict, individuals, families, groups, political leaders, or countries.

- Putting aside the judgement of the false self, we declare with our true self and with Christ the innocence of others because Christ has restored everyone to their original innocence. By his cross and resurrection he has redeemed the world. People are divided or in conflict only because they live from their false self. They have not accepted who they really are in their true self, for they are innocent and redeemed.

- By declaring the innocence of others we are praying with Christ that they will accept God's gift of the innocence of the true self. At the same time we are reinforcing the gift for ourselves, dispelling the guilt and the tendency to judge that have accumulated in us from original sin, personal sin and social sin.

- People who complete these exercises report a great release from guilt and a new freedom to be themselves. Some reach such a level of freedom that they say: 'there's really nothing to forgive anymore.' They have achieved the blessedness or peak experience Christ promises to those who embrace this Beatitude of mercy: 'Blessed are the merciful: they shall have mercy shown them.'

***Invitation:*** *I can be free.*

# Inspired to be a Model

A French Jew, set free from a concentration camp in Germany by American soldiers, appeared to be in the very best of health. 'Were you on special rations?' asked a soldier. 'No', he said. 'I got exactly the same as everyone else.' This man stood helpless as the Nazis shot each of his five children and his wife. Then they took him to a concentration camp.

Soon after the shooting, God gave him an astonishing gift, allowing him to see clearly that he had a choice. He could decide not to forgive, becoming angry and embittered for the rest of his life. Or he could forgive and be free to live a full life. He chose to forgive. During his time in the concentration camp he devoted all his efforts to helping people to forgive, and to see meaning in their lives, in spite of all the horror, the starvation, suffering and death.

## SOME CONCLUSIONS:

- We feel humbled and inspired by this man's generosity, both in forgiving and in devoting his life to helping people.

- He saw both the choices and the consequences of those choices. He understood that it is the venom, not the snake-bite that kills. The bites or hurts that others inflict on us do us limited harm. It is the venom of anger, resentment and bitterness that we let loose in ourselves that does the real damage. This man took responsibility for the choice he had before. In the cruellest of circumstances, he has become a most outstanding model of mercy and forgiveness for the world.

  It is easy to imagine the loving relationships he must have cultivated, and the appreciation and gratitude he enjoyed as he encouraged and supported people.

- Forgiveness had a miraculous effect on his well-being, in spite of an appalling diet. This is an example of the blessedness, the abundance Christ promises, if we would embrace this Beatitude wholeheartedly.

- In a world of fractured relationships it is urgent that we all model mercy and forgiveness, doing what we can to bring harmony and peace to those in conflict or breakdown, and supporting those who are oppressed in any way.

- We are inspired by the rich quality of freedom, fruitfulness and fulfilment this man enjoyed, and by the model that he still is, inspiring us to embrace this Beatitude with an open heart.

***Invitation:*** *I pray: 'Lord, make me an instrument of your mercy and forgiveness.'*

# Abundant Divine Power

*'Blessed are the pure in heart, they shall see God.'*

*(6th Beatitude)*

- To be pure in heart means to be single-minded or focused. What would give us this gift of focus, make us single-minded? We simply take a stand, which means that when we have a need or a goal, we commit to having the need answered or the goal achieved.

- Mary is an outstanding example of someone who took a stand. Having seen a need at the wedding feast, when the wine ran short, she took a stand that Christ would do the necessary. She simply asked him to do something, and then left it in his hands.

- Many of us tend to live from expectations, setting ourselves up for disappointment and hurt, fear and worry. Parents, for example, can have expectations of their children. The alternative is to be a stand for what is best in them. As soon as parents take this stand they create sacred space, space free of expectations and shoulds, free of worry and anxiety. Children are now free to grow and develop, and be themselves. Christ has the space to do what is necessary in their lives. And parents have the space, the freedom, to encourage, support and guide their children.

- By taking a stand, we are trusting that Christ has both the compassion and the power to do what is needed. We need to ask as Mary would have asked, that is, with gentleness, patience and confidence.

- We become more committed in our stands by putting them in the Abundance Prayer, creating sacred space, not only for Christ to act, but also for us to do what is in our power to do. A stand is partnership: we do what we can, and then surrender, allowing Christ to act in his own way, and in his own time.

- A stand gives us a new freedom to be one's true self. By creating sacred space, we experience a freedom from fear and worry, a freedom of knowing that no matter what happens the compassionate Christ has everything under control. This freedom allows us to do what we enjoy most, which is to be loving and generous towards all. The fruitfulness we enjoy makes us makes us happy and fulfilled.

- A stand establishes a profound relatedness with Christ and his abundance of life, love and peace, making us co-creators with him. The five steps in the next page show us how to make our stands powerful.

***Invitation:*** *Stands make me free, fruitful and fulfilled.*

# The Five Steps

As we take a stand we create the sacred space for Christ to be miraculous just as Mary did, having asked him to do something when the wine ran out. The following five steps will prove helpful.

1. Listen with wonder and gratitude, listen with the heart, to the promises of Christ: 'All things are possible with God,' and: 'I am with you always', with you to be miraculous with your stands.

2. Tell Christ what your stand is, for example, 'I'm a stand for the power of love,' adding, 'I trust in you, O Lord. With all my heart I trust in you.'

3. Constantly visualise in detail that what you stand for, Christ has already granted: 'Everything you ask and pray for, believe that you have it already' (Mark 11:24). This means that, having taken a stand for love, see love filling the heart of each person, filling homes, schools, hospitals, prisons, cities, countries, the world. If you find it difficult to visualise, it is sufficient to be aware of the presence of love.

4. Bring much love, desire and passion to your stands, be they for material or spiritual needs, giving greater emphasis to the latter. St. Paul encourages us to 'Be ambitious: for the higher gifts' *(1 Corinthians 12:31)*, the gifts of compassion, gentleness, justice, mercy, peace, etc. – the values of the Beatitudes.

5. Feel wonder, excitement and gratitude for the way Christ is always miraculous with your stands from the moment you take them: 'As soon as I definitely take a stand, Providence (the hand of God) moves too.'

By applying the five steps to our stands, we create sacred space for Christ to be miraculous, and for oneself to be more committed, passionate and inspired in doing what depends on us.

**Invitation:** *I now take a stand and apply the five steps to it.*

# Examples of Stands

- Reading through the Gospels we are struck by the stand Jesus was for everyone. We are sustained each moment by his continuing stand: 'I am with you always.'

- We are borne along by our communion with Mary, our mother, and all the angels and saints, by the energy of divine love their stands generate for us.

- People who care take big stands, parents, as well as people in all walks of life.

- Those who have inspired us were passionate in their love for people and for life. They were powerful stands.

- What is my stand? What am I committed to? Is my life selfish, mediocre or going nowhere? Or could I take a stand that would deliver the three Fs of love: freedom, fruitfulness and fulfilment?

- St. Therese of Lisieux took a stand to be love deep down in the heart of the Church, generating great love for both the Church and the world.

- We think of G.B. Shaw's passionate stand: 'Life is a splendid torch and I want to make it shine as brightly as possible before handing it on to future generations.'

- Parents who took a stand for what was best in their children reported that relationships in their home were transformed.

- If we look at our own needs or those of family, friends, neighbours, parish or world needs, etc., we can easily find something we want to stand for. Why not be one with Christ in his great stand to fill the world with his love and peace?

- People sometimes complain of frustration or boredom. The reason could be that they have not lived, have not given themselves to life, to the needs of others. Fear of death could also arise from this failure to love. Taking a big stand resolves this problem.

- We are defined by our stands or our lack of them. That is why it is urgent to take a big stand. 'Fill the water jars to the brim,' Jesus said, that is, give your life to a major stand. A small amount of water signifies a small stand. A large amount signifies a big stand.

**Invitation:** *I commit to a lasting passion for a big stand.*

# The Genius of a Stand

Until I take a stand,

I'm hesitant,

sitting on the fence,

bored and ineffective.


If I am to use my gifts

and be creative and fulfilled,

I need to appreciate one elementary truth:

the moment I definitely take a stand,

at that very moment

Providence (the hand of God) moves too.


All sorts of things occur to help me

that would not otherwise have occurred,

if I had not taken this stand.


A whole stream of miracles flow from my stand,

raising in my favour

numerous unforeseen incidents and meetings,

and spiritual and material assistance

which no one could have dreamed

would ever come my way.

*(Adapted from W.H. Murray: A Scottish Expedition to the Himalayas.)*


Whatever you can do or dream you can do,

begin it.

Boldness has genius, power and magic in it.

Begin it now! (Take a stand now).

*(Goethe)*


**Invitation:** *I read and reread this inspiring page.*

# Powerful Beyond Measure

Our deepest fear
is not that we're inadequate.
Our deepest fear is that
we're powerful beyond measure.
It's our light, not our darkness,
that most frightens us.

We ask ourselves: Who am I
to be brilliant, gorgeous, talented, fabulous?
Actually, who are you not to be?

You are a child of God.
Your playing small doesn't serve the world.

There's nothing enlightening about shrinking
so that other people
won't feel insecure around you.

We're all meant to shine, as children do.
We were born to make manifest
the glory of God that is within us.
It's not just in some of us:
it's in everyone.

And as we let our own light shine,
we unconsciously give other people
permission to do the same.
As we're liberated from our own fear,
our presence automatically liberates others.

*(Marianne Williamson)*

**Invitation:** *I am a stand for the greatness in every person.*

# A Stand to Move the World

Stands move the world, none more so than the stand Christ was for the whole human race: 'That you may have life in abundance.' When we consider the scale of the world's needs, it is most urgent that we be one with Christ in his all-embracing stand for humanity: 'I am a stand, Lord, that you will fill the world with the abundance of your love.' Only a stand of this magnitude will do justice to the infinity of God's love, and best serve God's purposes and the world's needs.

As soon as we take this stand we create sacred space for Christ to be miraculous in countless ways throughout the world. Our own needs are also looked after. By thinking abundance and taking a stand for it, abundance will flow to us, manifesting powerfully in our lives – 'It is in giving that we receive.'

We make this stand work powerfully when we desire God's abundance of love and peace for the whole world and for each person, when we continually picture this abundance filling the world and each person, and when we feel passion, excitement and gratitude for the miracle of so much abundance already present and of so much more to come.

It is important that we think big, seeing a vision of God's love erupting in such volume that it reaches the ends of the earth. And that we see a pandemic of God's peace spreading across all the continents of the world. The stand really works when we picture the gentle light of the risen Christ surrounding the planet and each person, dissolving all the negative forces, healing and uniting people in bonds of harmony, justice and peace.

We can be inspired by the example of St. Therese of Lisieux, whose stand was 'to be love deep down in the heart of the Church'. Her stand, and the millions she inspired, played a major role in renewing the Church and the world. We can be in action with our stand simply by holding the world in our sacred space in the Abundance Prayer, allowing our love to flow to it, and allowing Christ to be miraculous everywhere.

We do what we can to bring God's abundance to people, and we trust that Christ will do the rest. We trust that he will constantly turn 'water into wine', inspiring countless people to be open to love and to give love. That is why we can declare with the utmost confidence: 'I am a stand, Lord, that you will fill the world with the abundance of your love.'

*Invitation: I love my stand like a new born baby. I say it often in my heart. I feel passionate, grateful and inspired. I picture abundance everywhere, and in each person. I hold people and the world in my sacred space. I share my stand with like-minded people.*

# Stands or Expectations?

We take stands because we are inspired by love to make a difference in some way in the lives of people. We can be very focused at first but later lose our enthusiasm. Then our false self takes over, and our stands cease to be stands, becoming obligations, burdens and expectations we have of ourselves and others. They become more things we should do because we feel we have to.

As with everything in the abundant world of God and the true self, love is the motive and inspiration. Love keeps our stands alive with passion and focus, with patience and commitment. We discover a new freedom to be, at one with Christ and the true self in each person

When love is present nothing is too much trouble. We never stop to count the cost, but give freely and generously of ourselves. The fruits are enormous. Greatness is born in us. Our gifts and talents have the freedom, the space and scope, to be used in the loving service of others, increasing our fruitfulness, our contribution to making the world a better place. We achieve much and are very fulfilled. Wonder and gratitude are constant companions.

We see the evidence of what a powerful stand can achieve in the lives of such as Mother Teresa, Mahatma Gandhi and Nelson Mandela. And we also see it in the lives of those who have inspired us, people who seem ordinary but whose stands made them extraordinary.

The great choice is to allow our lives to be run by expectations or to take stands. The false self, living in the boxed-in world of scarcity, has many expectations. As God is pushed out fear takes over, and we settle for a life of survival and mediocrity. The true self, alive with passion for what love can do, is always an unshakable stand for love . The possibilities are enormous, and our lives never cease to expand with wisdom and understanding, with love and generosity.

Expectations control, stands create sacred space to risk, explore, make mistakes and learn from those mistakes. Expectations not met cause disappointment, hurt, anger, frustration and suffering. Stands see breakdown as an opportunity to learn, to trust, to communicate, to support and to renew our stands. Expectations box us in, prevent growth, and leave us fearful, anxious and immature.

Rather than accepting that we are victims of circumstances, having no say in our lives, we create the world we want to live in by taking stands. Stands build relationships with God and people, creating communities of love, harmony and peace. Stands awaken and enliven us with wonder and gratitude, making us abundant with freedom, fruitfulness and fulfilment. Failure to take stands leaves us in fear and scarcity.

***Invitation:*** *I pray that I will always be passionate with my stands.*

# Our Power to Transform

Take a stand for transformation.

Thrill to your greatness.

Awaken to Christ-consciousness.

Use your gifts

To express the power of your vision.

Share your stand for a transformed world.

Transform through prayer,

Transform through love,

Transform through surrender to the Spirit.

You are a free, immensely powerful source

Of divine life and transformation.

Delight in it,

Surrender to it,

Belong to it.

Focus day and night

On your power to transform,

And you will witness miracles

All around you, everywhere, in yourself.

Being this stand is the new freedom,

the new abundance,

the new happiness in Christ.

Be inspired!

Know that every stand

generates transformation.

**Invitation:** *I know my stands will transform.*

# Peace-making: An Exquisite Gift

*'Blessed are the peacemakers:*
*they shall be called sons and daughters of God.'*
*(7th Beatitude)*

Peacemaking consists of being a field of peaceful energy, of helping to resolve conflict and injustice, of deepening the peace already present, and of removing any obstacles to peace. We may not see ourselves as having any special gift for peacemaking, but as we live each of the Beatitudes, our hearts constantly expand with peace. As we become peaceful we aoutomatically become peacemakers.

As gentleness, for example, takes hold of us, we become great peacemakers, not so much by what we do, but by who we are. All we need to do to be peacemakers is to let go and surrender, allowing God's abundant peace in us to flow freely to every person, and to the whole world. There are times, of course, when we need to engage actively with people who are in conflict in order to bring about peace.

We are greatly inspired by observing Jesus, the Prince of peace. At his birth the angels announced to the shepherds: 'Peace to people of goodwill' *(Luke 2:14)*. Goodwill, therefore, is what allows people to partake in the peace of Jersus, and that includes those who have no religious faith, but who live lives of love and commitment.

During the thirty years Jesus spent in the anonymity of Nazareth, he was teaching us that peace is primarily something to be. Great peacemaking is possible only when we are at peace with ourselves, when we love the world, and when we surrender to Jesus and the abundance of his peace.

Encountering the divine peace in Jesus must have been an overwhelming experience for the disciples. No wonder they left everything and followed him. We can have a similar experience of peace in our encounter with Jesus. When others experience this peace in us, they will be drawn to Jesus and his peace. And so peacemaking is first of all, something to be, it is a matter of simply surrendering to peace, of being peace. We are automatically great peacemakers when our hearts are at peace.

After his resurrection Jesus always greeted people with the beautiful words: 'Peace be with you', showing how much he desired to give us his peace. We can be inspired by the promise of this Beatitude: peacemakers have the exalted status of being sons and daughters of God. We thank you, Lord, for the miracle of your presence, and the exquisite gift of your peace. We pray with St. Francis, the great apostle of peace, Lord, make me an instrument of your peace.

***Invitation:*** *My heart is constantly expanding with the peace of Jesus.*

# Peace-making: The Way Forward

If we are to be consistent in our peace making we need to embrace what is called 'the consistent ethic of life' which rejects the following. (Notice how each one violates justice, which is why there can be no peace without justice).

- Rejecting the violence of not treating each person with the respect their dignity deserves as priceless words of love spoken by God.

- Rejecting the violence of capital punishment, abortion and euthanasia.

- Rejecting the violence of accumulating needless wealth, and of not sharing our time and resources with others, but being content and happy with a simple lifestyle.

- Rejecting the violence of weapons of mass destruction in war.

- Being a stand against the injustices in society which cause disadvantaged groups to react violently.

- Rejecting the violence we do to the earth when we use up resources with little concern for the rest of creation either now or in the future. The native American Indians, for example, keep the seventh generation in mind for all important decisions.

## THE PEACEMAKER'S WORLD-VIEW

The committed peacemaker looks at the world with a very inspiring attitude:

- I see the whole human race as one family.

- I desire that every person be cherished as a priceless word of love, spoken by God.

- I desire that every person live in freedom and justice, harmony and peace.

- I desire the eternal bliss and ecstasy of heaven for all persons.

- I am one with Jesus in his passion to draw all persons into God's kingdom of love, and peace.

*Invitation:* Lord, make me an instrument of your peace.

# The Power of Non-Violence

We might wonder why Pope John Paul would say that Mahatma Gandhi, a Hindu, was his great model of peace and non-violence. Did he not have St. Francis and many other outstanding examples of peace in his own tradition? To understand Gandhi, we need to appreciate the scale of his achievement. He had a great passion to free his country from British rule. Having a deep love for Jesus and the teaching of the Gospels, he used to meditate on the Beatitudes. One day God gave him a peak experience where he saw that the British could be made to leave India through the power of peaceful resistance, or what he called, non-violence.

India had a population of three hundred and fifty million people at the time, and he succeeded in convincing the vast majority that a persistent campaign of non-violence would achieve independence for the country. The British were the enemy but Gandhi had deep respect for every person, because of which, he was vehemently opposed to the shedding of even one drop of blood. The power of his stand was such that the British had no alternative but to depart. His achievement stands as one of the greatest miracles ever known. Gandhi inspired Martin Luther King to take the American civil rights movement along the same road of non-violence. The results were stunning as Dr. King himself became an outstanding model for his followers. He is credited with steering his people past a bloodbath. Today he is seen as a great apostle of non-violence and continues to inspire many who hunger for justice. Nelson Mandela, in his fight against apartheid, was inspired by both Gandhi and King.

Non-violence is the very marrow of the Gospel, a necessary pre-condition if we are to love like Jesus, unconditionally. Jesus was totally opposed to violence. He was upset when the disciples wanted him to rain down fire and brimstone on the Samaritan town. And he told Peter to put away his sword when the soldiers came to arrest him. He chose to combat hatred and aggression through gentleness, emphasised in the image of the lamb as he accepted death without complaint. He surrendered freely and humbly to his destiny, to the will of his Father. Rising from the dead, he has become the great power in the world until the end of time.

Each of the Beatitudes prepares and equips us to live the Gospel of peace and non-violence. Reflecting daily on the Gentle Lifestyle, with its power to touch us deeply, we become fearless in the face of intimidation and violence. The urge to blame, complain or worry, etc., gives way to a loving acceptance of life and people. The non-violence of Jesus means that we see no one as an enemy or as an inferior. Inspired by the many models of non-violence, and empowered by the presence of Jesus, we can give our lives to non-violence.

***Invitation:*** *I embrace non-violence as a supreme value.*

# Transforming the Impossible

**'Blessed are those who are persecuted in the cause of right:**
**theirs is the kingdom of heaven.'**
*(8th Beatitude)*

Those who practice Christianity have always attracted hostility and violence. Countless followers of Jesus have been persecuted, tortured and martyred in the history of Christianity. Massive numbers have been killed in the last century alone.

From a human point of view this Beatitude would seem impossible. No one would relish the prospect of persecution, though many saints longed for what is called the crown of martyrdom. To understand this Beatitude it needs to be said that we are more than human: we are spiritual beings having a human experience. Moreover, we have Jesus and his peace in us. That means that we are empowered to live a life of non-violence. We can respond to blame, ill-treatment, insult, slander or persecution, with gentle, persevering love. We can even love our enemies, overcoming violence with non-violence.

Many people suffer great anguish as they struggle to give meaning to the pain of life. It seems nothing short of a miracle that they so often succeed against the odds. What sustains them is a sense of mystery, a hidden strength, a deep spiritual current. The mystery is Jesus and the source of this strength is Jesus, intimately present in spite of so much pain and darkness.

The prayer of an unknown Jewish prisoner at Ravensbruck concentration camp, left by the body of a dead Jewish child, typifies the meaning and power of this Beatitude:

'O Lord, remember not only the men and women of good will, but also those of ill will. But do not remember all the suffering they have inflicted on us; remember the fruits we have bought, thanks to this suffering - our comradeship, our loyalty, our humility, our courage, our generosity, the greatness of heart which has grown out of all this, and when they come to judgement let all the fruits which we have borne be their forgiveness.'

Could I write this letter? The true self in me says 'yes', the false self says 'no'. When Nelson Mandela, unjustly imprisoned, was put in solitary confinement his immediate response was: 'it's an opportunity'. Mandela had trained himself to see the opportunity in everything difficult or painful. The awareness of the true self tells us that Jesus is always with us, always giving us whatever it takes. So we can turn anything, no matter how difficult, into an opportunity. We can declare with St. Paul, 'I can do all things through him who strengthens me.'

***Invitation:*** *I learn to see opportunity for good in all of life.*

# Resilience: A Great Power

The mindfulness of true self awareness sees opportunity in everything. For anyone who practices mindfulness, it will be relatively easy to recognise opportunity when life is going well. But when people experience cruelty or loss, opportunity can be hard to see. Imagine a large heap of foul-smelling manure dumped at one's front door. Many would react with anger and upset. A gardener however, would be delighted, and would welcome the surprise gift. Knowing that the soil would be very enriched by the manure, they would look forward to a crop of the highest quality.

A young woman lived in the same house as her mother-in-law who was constantly demanding and abusive. Having considered her options, the young woman decided to take none of the abuse personally, adopting instead an attitude of kindness towards her.

By responding in this way she turned the manure of aggression into rich fertiliser for the soil of her life. She learned great patience and acceptance, and compassion for the pain in this woman that caused her to behave as she did. She now sees that her mother-in-law gave her a most valuable opportunity. The gift of resilience was a great power in maintaining her attitude of kindness, turning potential pain and resentment into opportunity.

Resilience is the strength that enables us to maintain attitudes of love when adversity arises, and to bounce back whenever we give in to anger, impatience, worry, etc. Resilience or fortitude is a gift of the Holy Spirit that we need to strengthen. We build it by taking advantage of the opportunities that arise daily, and also by reflecting each evening on the events of the day.

Did I see opportunity? Did I react negatively or respond in love? Was I aware of the gift of resilience and the choice I had to use it? We can also build resilience by thanking God for this gift. The more grateful we are, the more the resilience grows. By reflecting daily in this way we register our successes, bounce back when we fail, and add to our store of good memories. Our awareness of the Holy Spirit with us also grows, and we keep learning to recognise and use the opportunity whenever adversity arises.

And so we fertilise our lives with the pain, the manure, of every opportunity. As the resilience grows, we achieve a deeper experience of the three Fs of love, becoming more free, fruitful and fulfilled. A strong resilience is a very necessary asset in the living of this Beatitude. In the face of life's pain and hurt, we have everything to gain by building resilience of mind and heart.

***Invitation:*** *I value each opportunity to build resilience.*

# Stress, an Opportunity

Stress plays a major role in the lives of modern people. The following example is typical of the difficulties many face in today's economic climate. 'I have so many things to do. I get so stressed out. Surely life wasn't meant to be like this.' People are unavoidably busy with children, jobs, distances to travel, the worry of a mortgage, jobs at risk and a future full of uncertainty. Pressures such as these can make people feel so trapped that stress is inevitable.

A certain amount of stress is necessary, sharpening our concentration and keeping us focused. Stress is damaging, however, when the burdens of life are just too much, or when we react with anger, worry or anxiety to the fears and threats, real or imagined, that we are faced with. Mental, emotional and physical health suffers. Sleep is affected, the immune system is weakened, heart, cancer and other diseases are triggered, depression sets in. The balance and harmony of mind, feelings, body and spirit are upset, relationships are strained, and anxiety becomes a way of life.

The absence of God, low self-esteem and belief in scarcity, are major factors that increase stress levels. 'I'm afraid I won't be able to cope. I worry about what might happen.' When we think like this we do so with the false self. This thinking can easily take over our lives, causing us to feel deeply stressed. We do, however, have an option that will empower us. We can choose to think with our true self, giving us an abundance of what we need to turn every situation, no matter how grim, into an opportunity.

We grow into this awareness through the regular practice of one or more of the tools we have been discovering. Daily prayer creates the sacred space for God to sustain us, giving us the wisdom and the strength to find opportunity in the difficulties that arise. Awareness of the nearness of God also grows by speaking hope: 'God is good', 'all will be well', 'it's easier to trust than to worry.' Relying on our resilience is another great transformative power, replacing stress with strength, patience and confidence.

We can find great help in the Abundance Prayer. By creating sacred space we allow the love to flow to the person or situation that is causing the stress, sacred space also for Jesus to do what is necessary. The practice of wonder and gratitude give us the feeling that nothing is ever an insurmountable problem. We become so focused on the gifts of life that we have less time to be stressed. As we live the Beatitudes, stress dies in the presence of love. Trust in Providence grows as love grows, and we achieve an inner peace and balance that is the antidote of stress.

***Invitation:*** *I use the Abundance Prayer whenever I feel stress.*

# Testament of Dom Christian de Chergé

If it should happen one day — and it could be today — that I become a victim of the terrorism in Algeria, I would like my community, my Church, my family, to remember that my life was given to God and to this country, and to accept that the One Master of all life was not a stranger to this brutal departure.

I would like them to associate this death with so many other equally violent ones. My life has no more value than any other, nor any less value. I have lived long enough to know that I share in the evil which seems, alas, to prevail in the world, and even in that which would strike me blindly. I would like, when the time comes, to have a place of lucidity which would enable me to beg forgiveness of God, and of my fellow human beings, and at the same time to forgive with all my heart the one who would strike me down.

I could not desire such a death. It seems to me important to state this. I don't see, in fact, how I could rejoice if the people I love were indiscriminately accused of my murder. I know the contempt in which Algerians as a whole can be engulfed … For me Algeria and Islam are something different. They are a body and a soul. I have proclaimed it often enough, I think, in view of and in the knowledge of, what I have received from it, finding there so often that true strand of the Gospel, learned at my mother's knee, my very first Church, and precisely in Algeria, and already respecting believing Muslims.

My death, obviously, will appear to confirm those who hastily judged me naïve or idealistic: 'Let him tell us now what he thinks of it!' But these must know that my insistent curiosity will then be set free. This is what I shall be able to do, if God wills: immerse my gaze in that of the Father, to contemplate with him his children of Islam as he sees them., all shining with the glory of Christ, fruit of his passion, filled with the gift of the Spirit whose secret joy will always be to establish communion, and to refashion the likeness, playing with the differences.

This life lost, totally mine and totally theirs, I thank God, who seems to have wished it entirely for the sake of that joy, and in spite of everything. In this Thank You which is said for everything in my life, from now on, I certainly include you, friends of yesterday and today, and you, O my friends of this place, besides my mother and father, brothers and sisters and their families, a hundredfold as was promised.

And you too, my last–minute friend, who will not know what you are doing. Yes, for you too I say Thank You and this A-Dieu – to commend you to this God in whose face I see yours. And may we find each other happy 'good thieves' in paradise, if it pleases God, the Father of us both … Amen.

# Jane's Story

- I am told that I am dying ... I am not angry or bitter. I am in surprisingly good spirits. I joke, I laugh. It has not affected me in the sense that I'm depressed. I've even been told off for not being depressed.

- I do have my days of sadness – but not depressant sad – a sort of pleasant peculiar sadness more filled with a warm sort of lover and tenderness, like a soft rain. How marvellous. My spirit, you see, is very strong at the moment.

- I can't be bothered to be ill. I am determined. My resilience is like the iron hand in the velvet glove. ... Like a running gushing brook, flowing within me. Elusive, magical, enchanting.

- I will go to God. Whatever time I die I will go to God. ... I love people. I care for them. ... But I am me. I am only eighteen years old. Such a faith, such a love, I will have it forever. For as long as I live and then until eternity. It will only be in death that I will truly live.

- I see visions of darkness, winding pathways to a bright effervescent light. I see meadows, lush, green, mellow. I see these pictures as others would see their own memories. ... How can I see all this and be depressed, upset, alone? Why should I be miserable when I need not be? At least I am happy. I would do anything for my friends.

- I have no fear. It's not anything I have done. It's love that gave me this illness. Love. A special gift has been given. I need to be special to cope with it. My life has been blessed, enchanted, hanging in the balance of yesterday, today – forever.

- I am the luckiest woman in the world. ... I am not at all brave. I am terrified. And then I think of God and his warmth glows within me like a lukewarm sponge of peace and love.

- Some people search all their lives. And now my time has come to reach high into the skies. And finally – a star shines on me. And finally – I can touch eternity.

© *Jane O'Shaughnessy, died March 1993, of leukaemia, aged 18. This is an extract from her diary.*

**Invitation:** *'The sure hope of glory' comforts and inspires me.*

# A Disciple's Prayer

Jesus, Lord and Master, Friend and Saviour,
I praise and thank you
for the joy and privilege
of being your disciple.

I am a stand that all things are possible
through the power of your loving presence.
I trust that you are miraculous
with the stands I take.

Empty of negative concerns,
I delight in the vision of your abundance.
I bring silence and attentive listening
to the mystery of life as it unfolds,
I use the gift of committed speaking
to pray, to empower and to transform.

Acknowledging my broken, sinful condition,
I surrender to your healing touch.
I delight to make compassion a way of life.
I rejoice at the wonder of your gentle love,
so very abundant.

I stand for justice,
for the precious gift of every person,
unique, priceless and exquisite.
Healed and reconciled by your tender mercy,
I discover a special joy
in bringing this mercy to the world.
I open my heart in gratitude
to the miracle of your pure, single-minded love.

I respond to every opportunity
to be non-violent, your peacemaker.
I trust that you will be my strength,
no matter what suffering life brings.
Thank you, Jesus, for the peak experience,
the joy and privilege of being your disciple.

# Daily Bread

*Lord, in your abundant compassion, give us this day:*

- The bread of re-penting, re-thinking, so that we may have thoughts of love and compassion for every person.

- The bread of re-specting, seeing beauty and goodness in every person and in everything God has created.

- The bread of appreciating that we are constantly expanding possibilities for more and more wisdom and love.

- The bread of making wonder and gratitude our constant companions as we engage with the non-stop miracle of life.

- The bread of listening with the heart, with sensitivity and compassion, for the pain, fear and anxiety in others.

- The bread of speaking words of love and encouragement, to heal and enrich people in their pain and insecurity.

- The bread of compassion and tears for the pain and darkness of the world, and the grief of each person.

- The bread of gentleness towards the mystery of oneself, the mystery of every person, and the mystery of everything God has created.

- The bread of hunger and thirst for justice for every person, each a priceless word of love spoken by God.

- The bread of mercy, forgiveness and a generous heart.

- The bread of peace–making, delighting to reconcile and unite people in bonds of justice, harmony and peace.

- The bread of patience, strength and resilience in the face of whatever trials life may bring.

- The bread of a passionate stand for every person, that each will experience your abundant love, and be drawn into your kingdom.

# Freedoms That Inspire

- Inspired by the vision that 'all things are possible with God', we become more and more alive with passion for the possible.

- Declaring ourselves a stand for the reality of Christ and his abundant love, we enter into a deep relationship of trust and surrender with him.

- Delighting in the generosity of Christ, we are a stand that every person will experience the abundance of his love.

- Inspired by Christ always with us, and by what love can do, we step out in great confidence to bring justice and peace to the world.

- Inspired by the stunning rewards of the three Fs of love, freedom, fruitfulness and fulfilment, we avail of every opportunity to let our love flow to every person.

- Rejoicing that our true nature is to be free spirits, rejecting the culture of excess and addiction, we delight in the freedom of a simple lifestyle.

- Bringing wonder and gratitude to the adventure of life, the mystery never ceases to unfold with surprise, and discovery, with beauty and goodness, with celebration and peak experience, and with generosity to respond to the opportunity of the moment.

- Inspired by the presence of Christ, we can turn everything difficult or painful into an opportunity, the fertiliser that makes life fruitful.

- Using the gifts of humour and cheerfulness, especially in times of difficulty, we bring a new dynamic to our own lives and the lives of others.

- Celebrating that 'all will be well, and all will be well, and all manner of thing will be well' because God is always bringing good out of evil: 'Where sin abounded, grace abounded all the more.'

- Comforted and strengthened by 'The sure hope of glory', we make friends with death, our intimate sister, surrendering to the hand of Providence, drawing all people into the kingdom of heaven.

# The Joys of Love

## Freedom

## Fruitfulness

## Fulfillment

# Attitude

The longer I live, the more I realise
The impact of attitude on life.
Attitude to me
Is more important than education
Than money, than circumstances.

Attitude is more important
than failures, than successes,
Than what other people say or do.
Attitude is more important
Than appearance, giftedness or skill.

Attitude will make or break a company …
A Church … a home … an individual.
The remarkable thing is
We have a choice every day
Regarding the attitude
We will embrace for that day.

We cannot change our past …
We cannot change the fact
That people will act in a certain way.
We cannot change the inevitable.

The only thing we can do
Is play on the one string we have,
And that is our attitude …

I am convinced that
Life is ten per cent what happens to me,
And ninety per cent how I respond to it.
And so it is with you …
We are in charge of our attitudes.

*(Charles Swindell)*

# From Scarcity to Abundance

Summarising what we have been attempting to do so far, we can say that we have discovered powerful tools or ways of building attitudes of love, and of strengthening our emotional intelligence. Used regularly, these values or tools empower us to move from the negative world of darkness, frustration and despair, to God's world which overflows with beauty and goodness, peace and joy, and love with its exquisite fruits of freedom, fruitfulness and fulfilment.

We may wonder why we make such slow progress in our journey towards a more abundant life? The answer lies in appreciating the darkness caused by negative conditioning, a darkness sometimes so deep that it can persist day after day, causing continual confusion and indifference, and usually leading to loss of confidence or depression. Like the saints, we learn to persist, beginning anew each day, using the tools that best resonate with us. Persistence defeats discouragement, the temptation to give up, which is our great enemy.

Christ came to us to be the light that will dispel this darkness: 'I am the light of the world. The one who follows me will have the light of life.' To follow Christ is to bring light to our lives by adopting his way of thinking, the be-attitudes, making them our blueprint for life. These attitudes give us new eyes, new awareness, to see the light that is always dawning, revealing the rich abundance of God's world, and inspiring us to reach beyond what we think we can do. 'We learn that with God all things are indeed possible.

A key power consists of remembering that we have a choice. We can choose to think and speak the new language of the Beatitudes: 'All things are possible'. 'I can', 'I choose', 'It's an opportunity', 'God is always with me, giving me an abundance of what I need', 'All will be well,' My Relationships are Great, My Health is Great, My Life is Great, etc. This language gives us quick and powerful results. It is the language that creates the sacred space to experience Christ and the abundance of his love, making the attitudes of love in us deeper and more established.

We make great progress into God's world as soon as we begin to accept and appreciate ourselves and others. We re-spect, see with the eyes of the true self, see ourselves through God's eyes: unique, priceless and exquisite words of love spoken by God. We open our hearts to the truth that we are: hand-crafted in God's own image and likeness.

Constant practice of some of the following tools moves us powerfully into the light and peak experience of God's world. These tools include welcoming the new day with wonder and gratitude, and continuing to use these gifts during the day so that they become our travelling companions, two sacred friends, opening the door to a deep sense of mystery. Other valuable practices include smiling, reverence, the Abundance Prayer, taking stands, using the Five Steps, listening with love and speaking constructively, creating and deepening loving relationships and communities of love. By so doing, we create much peak experience for ourselves and for others.

The gift of tears, when we allow them to flow, are very effective in healing life's pain and hurt. Tears also help us to leave aside our preoccupation with selfish miseries, including expectations and the desire to control. Because they allow the love to flow, tears set us free to make the world a better place. We now find ourselves standing in the shoes of the true self, at one with Christ. Our hearts expand with compassion for the world in its pain, suffering and darkness, and with mercy for the sins of humankind. We conclude that tears deliver the three Fs of love, freedom, fruitfulness and fulfilment.

Every moment of gentleness, resilience, peacemaking and perseverance, in response to rejection, hurt, conflict or grief, propels us further into God's world. We highlight especially the extraordinary power and gift of the Gentle Lifestyle. The discipline of re-penting (thinking) and re-specting (looking deeper) also have great value. As we embrace the new lifestyle with its clutter-free space, we discover that each of these tools, and each of the eight Beatitudes give us added power to experience Christ and his abundance, and deepen and strengthen our emotional intelligence.

All the above practices and attitudes train us to trust in and surrender to the process of God's healing, transforming grace, and to the hand of Providence guiding us ever so gently. As this happens we find ourselves in God's world, experiencing the blessedness, the new wine, Christ promises to those who would embrace the new attitudes, the new wineskins.

It would be a great advantage to create a small altar in one's home, lighting a candle once or twice daily. We could then spend some time in family prayer or personal prayer. This practice would bring enormous benefits to ourselves, our families and the world. The support of a small group is extremely helpful as we seek to generate and maintain momentum towards God and God's world, choosing to let our true self do our thinking and make our decisions. Guidelines for a small group, as well as a study group are included in the final pages'

Life is the training ground, and Christ our partner, in setting aside the old attitudes and embracing the new. Every moment is an opportunity to open our minds and hearts to his gentle presence, allowing him to inspire us to live lives of ever-deepening love and generosity. He will always reward us with a deep inner peace that only he can give: 'A peace the world cannot give, that is my gift to you.'

*Invitation: I am overwhelmed by the gift of God's love.*

# An Examination of Awareness

- Am I growing daily in my love and appreciation for the priceless gift of the eight loving attitudes, the eight Beatitudes?

- What key tools do I use daily to internalize the meaning and power of the Beatitudes, making them an essential part of who I am?

- I can practise being mindful, living in the present moment, doing everything with love.

- I can make gratitude a way of life.

- I can take responsibility for the choices I make, and the consequences of those choices.

- I can practise the Abundance Prayer often, especially morning and night.

- I can live The Gentle Lifestyle which summarise the eight Beatitudes.

- I can listen with an open compassionate heart.

- I can speak the language of abundance: God is always with me, God is good, all will be well, it's an opportunity, I can, I'm always thanking God for his love and generosity, and for his countless gifts.

- I can make a habit of looking for opportunity in everything, especially when difficulties arise.

- I can read and reflect on a page of this book daily, and apply it to my life.

- I can have a hunger for justice, supporting people as best I can.

- I can be a peacemaker in my daily relationships

- I can give special attention to the stands I take.

- I can open my eyes constantly to the beauty and goodness of every one and every thing, and be nourished.

- I can commit to the gift of daily meditation.

# Guidelines for a Small Group

People report that they find the Abundance Prayer much more powerful in a small group. The experience inspires them to make the prayer a constant habit in daily life. Having shared the Abundance Prayer with others, one can then set up a small group. The group decides how often to meet, ideally, once a week. For the sake of continuity and the convenience of those who may not always attend, it is best that venue, day and time be always the same.

1. Requirements: a lighted candle, symbolising the presence of Jesus, on a small table placed in the middle of the room, surrounded by a circle of chairs, one for each member of the group.

2. Sacred music, is played for 10 to 15 minutes to help people to slow down and get into a receptive space. The music is playing as people arrive, no greetings, no talking.

3. The recording of the Abundance Prayer is then played, followed by ten minutes of silent meditation. The time may be lengthened gradually by the group to twenty minutes. To come out of the meditation, the leader/timekeeper begins the Our Father.

4. Anyone who wishes the group to pray for a specific intention says briefly what the intention is, while the group hold it in their sacred space. A pause needs to follow each intention to give the group time to pray for the intention.

5. A page from the book can be read.

6. Circle Prayer, spoken slowly, with pauses. Group sits in circle, left hands facing up, right hands facing down, resting gently on the palm beside them. We close our eyes gently, drop our shoulders and relax. We're aware of the heart of each person wide open, with a great flow of compassion coming to us from each one. We are aware that we're no longer alone. Feel accepted, feel loved, feel supported. Jesus in each of us is uniting us all as one.

   This is an experience of Jesus being the vine and we the branches. The more we can let go and relax, the more we allow ourselves to be healed and nourished by this great flow of compassion. Feel wonder, feel gratitude at the miracle that is taking place. May each of us become the person God intends us to be, alive and abundant, at one with Jesus in his love for the world.

# Guidelines for Group Study

- The group, meeting preferably once a week, prepares by reading and reflecting on one page daily, asking what the page is saying to them, and applying it to their lives. It would be good to take a few notes to bring to the group.

- The meeting may begin with the Abundance Prayer, which can be said or the CD played. (A free copy can be downloaded from www.theabundanceprayer.com).

- The leader emphasises that there is no discussion, only a sharing of what the pages mean, or what help each person gets from it.

- The leader begins by sharing what they got from the prepared page, and then invites the group to do the same, giving each person the opportunity to share.

- When the last person has shared, the leader encourages the group to spend time each day reflecting on the next page for the coming week.

- The meeting may conclude with the shorter form of the Abundance Prayer.